Healing Out Loud

Healing Out Loud

DIANA MEDINA

Copyright © 2021 Healing Out Loud.

All rights reserved. No part of this publication may be reproduced, distributed ut the prior written permission of the publisher, except in the case of brief quotations embodied in critical reviews and certain other noncommercial uses permitted by copyright law. For permission requests, write to the publisher, addressed "Attention: Permissions Coordinator," at the e-mail address below.

davina@alegriamagazine.com

Library of Congress Control Number: 2021917160

ISBN: 978-1-7361496-9-0

Published by Alegria Publishing
Book cover and layout by Sirenas Creative

DEDICATION

Milagro:

This book is your sibling.
I hope the world loves it as much as I love you.
Thank you for setting me free.
- Tu Mamá , en esta vida y la otra

Diana Medina

FOREWORD

I met Diana when I pledged the same sorority as her in college. Right off the bat, I got to know her for her prowess with the spoken word. At the time, that meant puns and jokes. Nothing snarky either. She just had a way of lifting the mood in whatever room she entered.

If you would have asked me to describe Diana in one word at the time, I would have said bubbly. Light, animated, spirited. In the years since we first met, I've learned that bubbly doesn't quite do Diana justice.

Diana's words come from a deep-cutting pain, from a need to heal, from undoing her past traumas and those of her ancestors. Her words still have that light, uplifting quality as they did so many years ago.

But if you were to ask me to describe her today, I would simply say "revolutionary."

Serena Maria Daniels
Chingona-In-Chief
Tostada Magazine

PREFACE

The pages in this book are the receipts of work I have done to become whole, navigate darkness, and come home to myself. When we are young we aren't taught what it means to be on a healing journey. Growing up as a first-generation American in a Mexican household as the youngest of eight kids, I certainly was not. In a household like mine, you get two kinds of responses from family when you get hurt: the people that say "andale por pendeja" or the people that say "sana, sana colita de rana" -while awkwardly patting your head. These two approaches taught me that getting hurt was my fault and that I should just get over it quickly.

As a kid, I would often get accused of "acting white" for having feelings and wanting to express them. Siblings would say things to me like "We're Mexican. We don't do that" or "This is real life not a tv show." As a result, I wrote secretly in notebooks and hid them under my bed. Sometimes someone would find my notebooks and read them out loud while mocking me. They'd call me dramatic or say I was acting. I hated being ridiculed for feeling so many feelings. I didn't want to hear them say "Qué tanto escribes? mejor ponte a limpiar" ever again. At the age of 18, I put the pen down, boxed up my notebooks, and focused on trying to become someone my family would approve of. Someone with a degree, a good job, a husband, a home, and a family. I didn't pick up a pen again until the age of 34 when the dark times that came with depression, miscarriage, anxiety, and divorce left me with no other choice. It was time to feel my feelings again, and I had sixteen years of bottled up wounds to process. Poetry became the way I dug myself out of that cage.

Healing Out Loud is a poetic celebration of the big, messy, grey area that lies between trauma and healing. An homage to the sights, sounds, and situations I encountered on my journey towards wholeness. This book is an exercise in describing all the things that they never show us in movie montages when pretty starlets get their life together. Like the pains our mothers and fathers don't talk about, or the processing we do in secret to deal with life's twists and turns, these are the things no one teaches us. This is the stuff we learn about by just hurting through it or surviving it. Poetry is the practice of reaching into yourself to pull out all of those things: the feelings, energies, burdens, and pains to describe them vividly. When you hold those things at certain angles, light hits them. They become shiny; You can reinvent them and yourself.

There is no creation without pain, no story without words, and no understanding without poetry. Poetry is the compass that always points towards perspective. I have learned many hard lessons after falling apart. But poetry is how I learned to take these lessons and turn them into fragments of healing. I continue to stumble and learn new lessons as I put myself back together. Some lessons are painful. Some are deep. Some are humorous. All of them are beautiful and worth documenting. I hope the words on these pages shed light for you on what it means to heal loudly and with intention. I hope this collection of poems serves as a catalyst for conversations you can have with yourself or with others. May these pages be a beacon on your path towards wholeness the way writing them has been a beacon on mine.

Diana Medina
Sacramento, California

Healing Out Loud

Diana Medina

Heal Out Loud

Grounded and firm I walk on this earth
Covered in the love of the wind's embrace
Smelling the earth for clarity
Feeling the sun for warmth
I am knowing, certain, and fierce
My pain relatable, my intuition unshakable
Less worried about where I've been
More concerned with where I'm going
My soul focused on learning to protect myself
From old monsters disguised as new possibilities
From my own anxious insecurities
From the weight of the world's expectations
Committed to make myself proud
Determined to heal out loud

April 13, 1994

I was 11 years old waiting to be picked up at school.
No one came to get me for a while until my sister eventually showed up.
After I climbed into the backseat of her car, she turned around to look at me and said, "Diana, Abuelita Kika died this morning. Ama and Apa just left to Mexico."

I nodded. I didn't know what to say.
We drove off in silence.
I felt a heavy sinking feeling in my gut.
Like my stomach was growling without making the actual sound.

When we got home, there was KFC for dinner.
My siblings were all there but no one talked about it,
at least not in front of me.
Little kids don't get to hear about those things.
No one talked about her or what happens when we die.
I thought about both as we ate.

I filled up on chicken, biscuits, mashed potatoes, memories, and unanswered existential questions until my stomach felt like it would burst.

I went to my room and laid in my bed feeling stuffed, sad,
confused, and unable to cry.
I thought about her with my eyes closed...
Her long, thick, grey trenzas, her checkered tops and long skirts
The lace head coverings she'd wear to church
Her colorful apron with the pockets where she kept money
and the key to her doll cabinet
Her wrinkled hands as they'd flip hot tortillas or touch my cheeks
They were overworked but always soft
Her smile as she told me each doll's name before she'd let me
pick one to play with
The sweetness in her voice when she'd call me "prietita."
The way she smelled like smoke, cinnamon, and pinol

I couldn't sleep under the weight of these memories.
I went outside to sit on my nephew's swing.
It was a baby swing, yellow, with black rope.
I was still small enough to squeeze into it.
I sat there in that cramped swing looking at the moon
I stared at all the palm trees in the distance
I hadn't noticed them until that day.
I saw her standing in one of them holding on to a thick branch,
Blue skirt, black and white checkered top, trenzas
shining in the moonlight.
She waved at me slowly for what felt like forever and then jumped
out of that tree.
I knew it was her, I knew she came to say goodbye to me
At that moment, my eyes filled up with the day's tears
I cried the hardest cry of my 11-year-old life that night.
I said "Abuelita" between sobs feeling the wetness covering my face.
I know now that this was the first time I felt grief.

Diana Medina

Muleicorn

If I was an animal
I would be a cross between a mule and a unicorn

A Muleicorn...the ultimate horse-like hybrid

Half-stubborn, strong, bearer of burdens, transporter of other's baggage.
A worker who goes hard as hell.

Half-flashy, elusive, and mythical creature with a distinct horn.
A moonlit fragment of magical flesh with an ability to shit rainbows.

The perfect combination of reality and fantasy.

Crossing Borders

Amá
Apá
I see both of you and I see myself
I see how your wisdom
is reflected in mine like a mirror
When you look at me you see
your best qualities staring back at you
in this stubborn, rebellious, loud mouth, black sheep of a package
I am overflowing with the essence of Natalia y Jose
Her gift with words
His determined work ethic
Her unshakeable conviction
His creative resourcefulness
Her attitude and sass
His humor and wit
All of it is also mine
All of it is also me
There is nothing about me
that you haven't had a hand in creating
I hear how your words tell me:
Stop, calmate, wait a minute, habla con dios, take it easy mija
But I also how see how your eyes tell me:
Echale ganas, feel things, vuela mija, god is guiding you
and I listen more to your eyes than I do to your words
You see my gut has always told me your dirty little secret
That your eyes are where your hopes and dreams for me live
and your words are where your fears and worries for me live
Your words yell at me
because you worry that you've created a monster
but your eyes...
Your eyes are beaming at me
because they are certain that you've created a warrior
We go through the motions of these disagreements as a formality
keeping the dance for parents and child alive
And in that dance I can see it
I can see your eyes betray your words

You can't hide it from me
You are me and I am you
I know what you really want
because I know what I really want
You want to stop time for both our sakes
You want to keep me a baby just a little longer
You want me to stay where you can see me and keep me safe
But you also want more
more than what you thought was possible for you
more than what your parents and grandparents could have imagined
And we have the same heart
so I know what I have to do
when your words cry out in fear
and your eyes glimmer with hope
Our hearts are just not a place capable of storing lies. Only these truths can exist there:
1 - That you deferred your childhood so you made sure I had one
2 - You knew the world would not be kind so you raised me with faith and courage and fear and worry to keep me vigilant
3 - We are monsters and every monster has to have a little warrior in them to be scary
4 - We are warriors and every warrior has to have a little monster in them to be strong
5 - Thanks to you the world is not ready for a woman as strong as me.
When I was born you cut the wings of your backs and gave them to me not knowing where in the world I am going to fly off to
or when I would leave
You armed me for a journey into the unknown with an endless supply of bendiciones and burritos
You agreed to stay exactly where you are so I can always find you when I've lost my way knowing all the while that my words will forget to say thank you but my eyes will always be grateful
I'm going to fly despite all of our fears because my words
promised your eyes I would
You crossed a border to give me this life and every day I ask myself what border do I need to cross to pay you back for that sacrifice?
Your eyes will see our dreams realized because where I fly, you fly and that is what these wings are for

Sister Friend

My rock
My mirror
we were seeds learning how to plant ourselves
we found acceptance and accountability in one another
In our words and actions always having our backs
Anchors tethering ourselves to our roots while we went off to explore the world
Rescuing one another from struggles
Challenging one another when obstacles were our doing
Questioning each other's choices in service of our higher selves

This Body

Finding comfort in my body is a violent journey. First there is the physical fight with the "must get skinny" mindset that society gave me. The one that tells me my belly and my boobs and that terrible double chin I get when I take a selfie at the wrong angle are wrong, inappropriate, unattractive, and undesirable.

Then there is the battle I fight with my own body. The one where I deprive myself of carbs and sugar and food cooked with my mother's love. Desperately committing to vanishing before my own eyes. All in the name being a single digit number on a pair of jeans. Just another victim of the diet industrial complex.

Then there is the battle I fight with the part of me that knows different. The part of me that looks in the mirror and sees curves and abundance. The part of me that sees a body that is hearty like a bowl of caldo on a cold day; and breasts that refuse to hide under baggy shirts because they insist on entering every room before I do; and hair that looks better messy because my follicles are so committed to authenticity that they refuse to be manipulated by my hands or hair products or a brush; and eyes that know pain intimately yet still choose to see light.

Through all of these fights, there is my skin. It is the container that holds me all together. Maintaining the boundaries of these inner battles I fight with myself. Glowing when I am in alignment. Itching or breaking out when I am not. Somehow always finding its own way to tell me the things I need to know when my brain doesn't want to listen to reason, or when my intuition is drowned out by my doubt, or when the expectations of others feel like obligations that I try and fail to meet.

Through it all, my skin steadily holds me together. Shrinking, expanding, glowing, bleeding, scarring, and healing. All for me. Down for the cause of my battle that day no matter what it is. If that isn't comfort I don't know what is.

Just a Mess

My doctor said "well it's just a mess in there" as she showed me pictures of my insides. It was a Tuesday morning. As good a day as any to feel empty inside. I saw the blood and the scaring and cysts. Then, she pointed to the small blob they had to remove to save me.

"So…what are my options now?" I asked.

"Well it's just a mess in there," she said again. This time with a shoulder shrug.

It was such a dismissive tone. As if my womb was a messy closet or a cluttered counter top. I felt fire welling in my insides. My ovaries were angry. And the more she talked, the angrier I became.

She started telling me all the ways my road to motherhood would be difficult now. How it would only be possible with fertility treatments because…

"Well… it's just a mess in there." She said it again and this time she pointed to my abdomen.

It broke me every time she said it. Never in my life had I seen someone brush off another's tragedy so casually. As if she was making sure my sadness didn't stain her coat. I wondered if this was how all doctors keep their coats so white?

I felt the burning inside me again. My ovaries were raging so hard. I could feel cysts filled with sass forming in new spots of me with every breath I took. It took all of my will power to not slap this doctor in the face for saying my reproductive system was a "just a mess."

Who would say that to someone whose body feels like a graveyard now? Did she not see how my hopes for family were now dead and buried in that mess? Can't a mess still be beautiful? That mess is attached to a human. A human who is now feels incomplete thanks to a destructive surgical womb remodel she administered. Did I not still have feelings? Did

I not deserve dignity and empathy in this moment? Do they not teach that in medical school?

I tuned her out around the time she started to tell me how hard it would be for my body to become pregnant again.

Growing up in a family where female fertility is the norm and giving my Mexican mother grandchildren before she dies is an expectation I have been reminded of every day of my life. This news, this conversation, and this doctor shattered me.

I thought: this will be the hardest thing to accept. My inconsolable uterus agreed.

Fixer Upper Womb

I don't know how to picture myself anymore. I struggle to accept incompleteness as part of my identity. I wake up hoping today will be the day it becomes a source of strength. But life has a way of testing those hopes when I scroll through Instagram.

Today one of my pregnant friends posted a lovely, artistic, and inspirational picture
of a female reproductive system. It was surrounded by flowers. All the parts laid out nicely: two ovaries and two Fallopian tubes. All beautifully symmetrical framing both sides of the uterus
like a set of stylish table lamps flaking a king size bed in a fancy hotel. The picture highlighted the beauty of the female design. A colorful and divine blueprint for the first home of humanity.
The first place a life grows in, sleeps in, eats in, breathes in, feels safe in.

Then there's my blueprint... my blueprint that is all fucked up... my blueprint that is "just a mess" according to my doctor. My blueprint looks like a terrible DIY home remodel job; the kind they would showcase on one of those HGTV shows as the before scenario,
the "don't let this happen to you scenario", the "we can fix it and increase its property value" scenario.

I imagine the two tall, dark, and handsome Property Brothers coming into my uterus with lights and cameras ready to take a tour of my botched reproductive system. Promising to remodel it into something worth living in. I would show them and the viewers my charming and quaint fixer upper womb. The Property Brothers would be walking around me making comments about the neighborhood I am in and all the ways they can improve my curb appeal. They'd talk about how my reproductive system has "good bones" and just needs "better use of space." They'd point out the problems that need fixing or hiding. The botched plumbing job where my Fallopian tubes are; one of them intact but deteriorated, the other missing completely. The hoarder style overpacked closets in my ovaries. The unfortunate lack of area rugs everywhere. Then they'd sidebar into a lecture for the viewers about how area rugs are amazing and a great way to really "define and ground your living space." The whole time they'd be ignoring the pain on my face. Ignoring the fact that I had spent years planning a housewarming party for a baby in this womb. It RSVP'd once but it never showed up.

They'd unveil their plans on how my womb would be transformed into a livable space. The real estate agent brother in the suit would go first showing me on the fancy computer simulation how he'd turn the space my missing fallopian tube left behind into a beautiful garden with plants and teak furniture and a BBQ grill and a water feature. He'd call it a lush space for me to relax and entertain. But I don't need a place to relax and entertain. I need a place to grieve and reflect. I'd say, "I don't want to throw BBQs in the part of me where something died." Then, the handy contractor brother in the flannel shirt would ask me, "well what can you entertain there? What can you see going in that spot?"

I'd tell them how right now I entertain hard and heavy thoughts there. I think of how all these states want to pass laws to define legal personhood insisting life begins at conception. How
other states are passing stricter and stricter abortion laws restricting access to that hard choice. I think that's so messed up. I have been in the place where your only option is to exercise that hard choice over your body. I have held friends who made that hard decision to not continue a pregnancy. These crazy white men want to take that choice from us.

I'd tell them how at the same time, I think about having been in the place where I got to see a tiny little speck on a monitor. A heartbeat that was not mine flickering and dancing inside of me for all of 3 minutes. I was not done being amazed by it when they unplugged the screen and hauled me off to tear that little flicker out of me in order to save my life. It was the most traumatic medical procedure I've ever experienced and the most beautiful 3 minutes of my life.
In my logical mind I know that wasn't a person, but in my heart… in my heart it was a life, a life I made. I never got to meet it or hold it or sing to it or look in its eyes or teach it how to ride a bike or play with it… all I got was 3 minutes with a speck on a monitor.

Then, I would ask the Property Brothers to build me a memorial in the space in my body where the little speck of life used to be. I'd ask them to plant grass in the shape of a circle just big enough for a bench and garden of cacti to surround it. Something green and beautiful and full of life that is also prickly and painful to touch. Something with sand and dirt and dead dry grass surrounding the rest of it so that death and life and green and dark can coexist side by side.
Because that is how it feels to have this womb now. It doesn't feel like a mess. It feels like a part of me died and the rest of me has to live with it.

I need this part of my womb to become a memorial. I need the grass to be next to the dirt
to remind me that sometimes the difference between dead grass and green grass
is just one turn and one step. I need the bench to sit on when the things I need to deal with come to visit me like my shattered dreams or my wounded ego or triggers from my past traumas. A place to sit and cry when grief comes to visit, and dream when hope comes to visit.
A place to get the hell up from to go live when life comes to visit. Maybe if I sit here at that memorial long enough perhaps I will eventually say enough prayers or write enough words or live with enough purpose to honor that little speck of life I never got to meet. Maybe each time I do, a new patch of grass will grow and extend into the dead and dry parts of me to fill them with new meaning or a positive spin on why this had to happen to me. Maybe if I sit here long enough, god or the universe will give me a logical explanation outlined in a detailed flow chart or PowerPoint presentation of why this loss was the bullet I was meant to take.

Then, the Property Brothers would look at me confused and ask about the cacti. "Why do you need so much cacti?" I would tell them how I need cacti because this plan may be stupid. We may plant new grass there that will still die and look exactly like the dead patches that were already there in the first place. In the event that happens, the cacti will be there ready to show me that life can still thrive in apparent scarcity and remind me that, just like them, I have everything I need to stay alive on barren land.

Maybe having this memorial designed by the Property Brothers in my imagination will give me peace. Maybe it will show my doctor that I am actually divine and not "just a mess." Maybe one day, a life can still live in this fixer upper womb of mine. Maybe the day that life moves in, they will see an ovary with a cyst for a chandelier and a missing tube on my left side of me and find it all quaint and cozy and charming and just perfect for them. Maybe that life will also see all those closets in my heart and throat filled to the brim with words and wounds that have not yet burst and use them as art to decorate the empty walls inside me.

Sana, Sana (the remix)

When I go to the spa
I think of the frog's butt
The only brown giggle
in the white old lady silence
Living my brightest life
in a bland steam room
Humming my favorite
mantra to higher self:

Sauna, Sauna
colita de rana
If your cabecita hurts a lot
have a banana
Or just go to the gym
today not manaña
Science has proven
it will help you in dealing
Help you with stresses
Help you with healing
Some say using treadmills
is better than feeling
lifting weights gives you power
when you raise them toward the ceiling
But if tomorrow you find
that you just don't want to go
have a taco and try the next day
No one but you has to know

Prayer for Evolution

In my darkness, please,
point me to the kernels of wisdom
that will shine when I hold them up to the light.

Guide me to the tables
where my soul can eat courageously,
exist bravely, and heal loudly.

Remind me of my roots and my scars
so they can become my strength
when lights dim and struggles come.

Help me accept the truths of truths:
that suffering is temporary,
that every path brings a lesson,
that wisdom is forever,
that I am imperfect and infinite,
broken and beautiful,
fractured and finally free.

Birth of a New Year's Resolution

I need to stop buying pastries for breakfast
they are so delicious
but now my jeans don't fit
I love my yoga pants
but I really miss my jeans
and truth be told
I haven't been to yoga in months
I should call them lazy pants

Quicksand

My sofa feels like quicksand
I am slowly sinking in to it
to run from my responsibilities
Work, bills, cleaning, errands
I don't want to do any of it
I used to enjoy it
I used to be on top of it
I used to try
Today I'm just heavy
I can't put my finger on why
The quicksand feels soft and warm
Like it's hugging my skin
Pulling it deeper and lower
into a comfortable paused place
Where time and feels all stand still
Where I can decide what is wrong or what is not
Where I can miss the movement I am avoiding

Apá

I am a full grown women pero
cuando mi apá me abraza
I shrink and I am transported
Otra vez, soy la chiquita de papa
a loving little girl looking up
at this tall strong gentle giant
whose shadow towers over me
as his arms protect me like treasure
that is the beauty and magic of mi apa
when we embrace, we go back in time

Worry vs Calm

I live a life where Worry and Calm
are playing a ruthless game of tetherball.
Worry keeps winning but the game won't end
and, true to form, Calm is just standing there
watching and waiting, I have no idea for what.
Worry goes all in seeing and attacking
whatever the ball represents without thought.
I wonder: How the hell can I make this game stop?
I pray for the day when I see the lines on the floor,
the pole in the ground, a ball on a rope, and have the power
to remember that despite these suggestions all around me
pushing me towards that never-ending game, I don't have to play.

Self-doubt is my homegirl

She is here and she won't leave
She is the part of me that is skilled
Skilled at staying small, skilled at being in the way, skilled at playing it safe
She sees me trying to heal and fears not having a role to play in my future
She is that homegirl who doesn't ever want to go to the party
but she also doesn't want me to go out without her
I prep us for our nights out with a series of annoying negotiations
I say: Let's just take a shower and see if you want to go
Let's just put on a dress and see if you want to go
Let's just let me do your hair and see if you want to go
Let's just put on your shoes and see if you want to go
Let's just get in the car and see if you want to go
She keeps me stuck... one foot in my future, one foot in my past
Moving forward slower than I want to, getting to parties later than I want to
All because I love her too much to leave her behind
Inside I wonder:
Can she stop being a fucking wet blanket?
Can she just get out of the car so we can go into the party?
Doesn't she want to evolve and grow with me?
Doesn't she see she will have a blast once we go inside?
She has been a loyal companion and confidant all my life.
How exactly do I break up with her?

Quiet vs Noise

When my quiet swims in your noise, my vibrations crash with your distractions.
How can I honor my stillness when you won't stop moving around me?
How can I be with my thoughts when you refuse to be with yours?
My thoughts and reflections need to breathe. Do yours want to drown?
You want me to smile and pretend your noise is welcome.
To act like the stillness I desire isn't quenching the thirst my higher self has for clarity and compassion.
To dive into your noise head first as if it was mine too.
But my vibration turns into an earthquake in my cells when the fault lines of my smile move to honor your request.
Is it easier for me to swim in your noise than it is for you to drown in my quiet?

Endaversary

He asked me for a divorce on a Monday morning
That day I went to work
I broke down in a meeting with my boss
She hugged me and we cried together
I paused my crying for a one-hour meeting
Afterwards I locked myself in an office to cry more
Then I paused my crying to supervise my team's 4-hour shift
When they left I cried at my desk
Then I cried in the elevator
Then I cried in the car on my way home
I paused my crying when I got home
So I could look strong in front of him

The Cost of Freedom

After telling me it was over you said,
"I don't know why I'm laughing and crying at the same time."
"I don't know either," I responded.
Inside I thought, perhaps you're laughing because
you finally have the freedom you wanted
and crying because of what it will cost you to get it.

Not married anymore

6 plastic storage containers, transparent with grey tops, exposing what happened here, inside: my entire wardrobe, all my toiletries in sloppy stacks, all the sexy underwear I stopped wearing years ago, and my books stacked neatly with titles facing out methodically packed to show themselves to the world.

Me putting boxes in the car, a cloudy blue Honda Fit with the seats pulled down, a big open space on wheels, plenty of room to transport a whole life, my forehead and face glistening with a combination of sweat and tears, and my shaking hands adjusting my sloppy bun.

You offered to help me, too little too late, as usual, I had already done most of the work.

Directions

I gave you all of me.
I just couldn't give you a baby.
So you discarded my incomplete fixer upper reproductive system
and found yourself a move-in-ready womb.
Trading in a wife for a baby momma
Giving up on the hard work of manhood and marriage.
Relying instead on convenience and cowardice to get yourself to your goal: fatherhood.

Meanwhile, my soul hears the spirit of the baby we lost.
It calls me mother every day.
I honor it by attempting to rebuild a new life among ruins.
Hoping one day to create a legacy worthy of its admiration.
If our baby knew where your soul lived maybe you would've heard it calling you father too.
But I suppose you can't give anyone directions to a place you've never been...

Finding Me

If you are looking for me
start with melancholy
Next, go to the center of moments
and merge to the start of meaning
Or look for me in the middle of something
when other things don't make sense
Then look in melodies, meals, and memories
You can't have any of these things without me
Without me, they are nonsense
Incomplete fragments of a life
Random letters on a page
and if all else fails at the end
Find me in awesome
I'll be there waiting... I promise.

One-Woman Dance Party

Under this light I dance with my past selves
It is the only way we can all be present and speak the same language
I dance with the 5-year-old little me
She has scabby knees, a sloppy ponytail, and hair in her face
Her brilliant brain is full of commercial jingles that she memorized
to block out the sounds of the adults that fight around her.
I dance with the 15-year-old teenage me, tears frame her skin in sadness
She is in shambles with a newly broken heart after laying eyes on the first
of many men that were not ready to love her only fully equipped to hurt her
I dance with the 21-year-old me hiding her beauty under baggy clothing
She punishes herself by keeping the world from seeing her
She is scared to take up space and her heart is filled with shame
her mother's prayers couldn't protect her from hands
intent on taking parts of her that she wasn't giving away
Together they hold hands and they dance with me as I am today
The one that I see in the mirror
The one that I struggle to trust
My eyes are watery with tears that flood out of my soul
for losing myself trying to build a life in a home not meant for us
Together we lay our broken parts on the floor
Sharing how we survived when we didn't feel whole
Music blasts as we do an autopsy on our pains
Dissecting decisions to mine for inner wisdom
Pulling out pearls from the deep perils we've endured
Conducting a forensic accounting of the virtues and gifts
That our fears embezzled from us so that we can restore our balance
So we can feel positive, abundant, beautiful, and strong
We hold hands and agree to meet again for this healing dance
A sacred one-woman dance party that will last the rest of our lives

Apology to myself

I'm sorry
That I'm too hurt to stay firm
That I am trying and failing
That I am not sure yet
That I don't always value my love
That I let my heart trust too quickly
That I allow kindness to get me in trouble
That I figured myself out too late
That I don't know the answers
That I have so many questions
That I feel so intensely
That I loved others more than myself
That I beat myself up for my shortcomings
That I allow kind faces to be my heart's kryptonite
I am so sorry

The Gift of Sabotage

Sometimes sabotage gives you certainty
Certainty then gives you control
Control then gives you relief
Relief is a break from the unknown
And the unknown is a place
we can't bear to stay in, so we sabotage

We sabotage ourselves
Our goodness
Our relationships
Our friendships
Our jobs
Our potential
We turn life into a series of self-fulfilling prophesies
Thinking this is what it means to be the writers of our own stories,
the forgers of our own paths, we focus on choices rather than chances,
Setting answers in stone rather than letting life surprise us

Tiny Cracks

The beauty of the universe is that it is filled with tiny cracks
Those cracks show us pieces of light in our darkest times
The tiny cracks of light take on many forms
They are in the deep breaths we take each day
They are in the lyrics of a song
They are in the sound of birds chirping
They are in the warmth of a friend's embrace
They are in the wrinkles of your smile
They are in the firmness of a hand being held
They are in the ticklish spots on our bodies
The spots that make us to respond to a lover's touch
Because we feel safe enough to bend and giggle
These things are expressions of resilience
They are gifts from our body that remind us we are alive
That we are wired to see light and be light in dark times
Even in moments of grief that make our life feel empty
These tiny cracks of light prove that we are not empty people
That we are capable of filling our own cup
That we are capable of seeing and being our own light
That we are able to hold pain and joy at the same time
After all isn't that why god built us with two eyes, two hands, and one heart?

Tiny Paper Cuts

I'm up again today.
Waking up on a couch
Aching body, aching heart
Everything is different inside
The world has no idea
I need to laugh again
I need to sleep in my own bed again
I need to remember how to sleep alone again
I have to teach myself new things again
Like how to not think about you
How to not worry about you
How to stop missing you
What kind of person misses someone who doesn't want them?
Who wants to relive that pain all the time?
There's a million tiny paper cuts on my heart.
They are in all the places that once welcomed you.
I have to learn how to feel right alone again
Why did you do this?
Why wasn't I enough?
Why was I too much?

Confessions of a recovering doormat

I may never allow anyone into in my spirit
the way I let you in.
I welcomed you into all of me with open arms.
You took the dreams I had of growing old with you and weaponized them.
Dangling affection in front of me as if I were a hungry street dog looking
for a sign of kindness to restore my hope in humanity.
Teasing and childish one more moment careless and entitled the next.
But there you were wiping your feet on my traumas as if they were your
personal doormat.
And there I was allowing it all to happen
thinking this is what it meant to be loved.

Useless

Calling you a piece of shit
would be an insult to shit
Shit would be deeply offended
at the idea of being a piece of you
Because shit is the same as manure
Manure helps grow things
Crops on farms, plants in gardens,
Manure fuels fires and ecosystems
People use, need, and want that stuff
So even shit has a purpose
You, on the other hand, don't

Glow

The moment I left you
My hair stopped falling out
My posture got better
My smile came back
My skin started to glow

People told me I looked sad but seemed lighter
freer, more alive, more like who I used to be
Their excitement was like being welcomed back from a long trip away

There are more nutrients in the air for me now
My pores and lungs rejoice knowing
They no longer need to sustain me on a diet of your toxicity
My nose is ecstatic that I will never smell your farts again

There is way more land I can cover
in the journey towards my dreams
now that I don't have to drag you along

My body knew your absence would be good for me
Long before my mind and heart accepted it
Way before my eyes stopped crying
This glow is my body's way of saying "I told you so"

The Seed We Planted

The seed she planted was precious.
A combination of good intentions,
belly laughter, and love.

The garden was eager
to share its greatness
The seed was resilient enough
to cling to life no matter where it landed.

The seed grew in the midst of storms
Until it got lost in the garden

When the garden tried to find the place
where the seed's first roots attached
It started a messy scavenger hunt.
Where the garden endured discomfort
parts of her were even cut down
as a sacrifice to save herself

She searched in the roots,
a new piece of the old seed
to save and replant
but growing that seed
was not possible on this new
narrower, rockier, ground.
The garden gave up.

No one had ever told her
gardens can grow anywhere.
All she needed was new seeds.

Ready, Aim, Fire

The beauty of being both
a poet and a woman scorned
is that my pen is my gat
and I am not afraid to fire it.

My bullets are made of
magical mixes of metaphors

My truth is manufactured in the
spaces of my heart that once held
undying affection.

My poetry is painstakingly prepared
with purpose and perspective
to penetrate fragile egos
masquerading as bullet proof vests.

My delivery can bury the bravados
of basic men under
alliterative avalanches of
awareness, anger, and anguish.

My lines and rhymes
holding them accountable
for crimes against my spirit.

My fast fingertips
type reflective responses
with bullets of quick wit
that never miss their targets.

Hell has never seen
and man has never felt
a beautiful fury like this.

Playing House

I don't know if what we had was fire
maybe we had our moments.
But I found comfort in the calluses of his hands
every time I'd feel them on my skin.

I found warmth in his arms on cold days.
Sometimes my humor found acceptance in his.
On hard days his aloof presence
gave me the illusion of good company.

There were enough lies in his words
to believe we were soulmates,
but enough truth in his actions to see
we were roommates; nothing more.

I felt deep loneliness in his presence
It was tragic but at least it was familiar.
What a convincing actor he was
going through the motions of marriage.

It was the longest game of house I've ever played.

Baby Momma DMs

I came face to face with my pain today
I was minding my own business
when your baby momma slid into my DMs

I asked why after all this time
did she message me
and interrupt my healing just to say hello

She told me you used her as a uterus donor
and left her to marry someone else.

She told me she was happy for me
because unlike her, I am free of you.
God blessed me with a clean break.

We filled in the blanks in search of clarity.
She told me the name of the bullet I dodged.

Some would call it crazy to put myself through such torture.
But it's not every day that a pain like this slides into your DMs,
I couldn't squander the chance to get some answers.

Human Kidney Stone

You were like a human kidney stone
that I painfully passed through my 20s
My child bearing years
My career building years
My soul-searching years.

Years I stayed small to make you happy
Years I stayed quiet to make you feel smart
Years I stayed blind to my own traumas to help you with yours.
Years I filtered you through my heart over and over
because I thought you had potential.

In the wake of your passage
I was able to deeply understand
what type of toxic male, entitled,
parasite of white privilege you were.

And just like a kidney stone,
I thought you were part of me until I passed you.
You were just a small pebble of waste
who made himself at home on my coattails.

Irreconcilable Differences

"Diana, there's a sheriff here to see you."
Everyone heard and started to whisper
as I walked to the front desk.
The sheriff handed me a brown envelope
inside was a grenade: divorce papers from you

I held that stack of papers in my shaking hands
I never knew paper could weigh so much
I was embarrassed and angry
Why did you do it this way?
Why not ask a friend to give them to me?
Why have a uniformed sheriff bring them to me here? To my job?
Why didn't you have the courage
to give them to me yourself?
like an adult

Did you want my coworkers to see me broken?
Was this part of how you wanted to torture me?

As I looked at the grenade on my desk
I read one phrase over and over
Irreconcilable Differences...
Irreconcilable Differences...
IRRECONCILABLE DIFFERENCES
I stared at the box next to it and the big "X"
in your smug handwriting

If divorce papers were honest
they would make you say the truth
They would make you put an "X"
in 100 boxes next to the phrase
"I refuse to take responsibility for giving up on this marriage"
I wished courts would require you
as the Petitioner filing this breakup paperwork
to own your reasons in writing.

I closed my eyes
and imagined
a long typed out addendum
written in blurry, old typewriter font
with boxes you would have to check off and initial
one after the other
of all the real reasons why
you really gave up on us:

It would say things like:
- Petitioner stood still while Respondent kept evolving
- Petitioner was too selfish to love Respondent through the hardest years of her life
- Petitioner wants children and Respondent can't have them naturally anymore.
- Petitioner was too afraid of the effort required of him on days when love became a choice and stopped being just a feeling.
- Petitioner's ego was threatened when he could no longer manipulate his way out of arguments with Respondent.
- Petitioner couldn't handle it when Respondent stopped coming home to him and started coming home to herself
- But, Petitioner would like Respondent to remember that he is still a good guy because he never hit her.
- Also, Petitioner hopes he and Respondent can stay friends because he feels entitled to use her energy, effort and time to provide emotional support.
- Finally, Petitioner's new girlfriend is already pregnant so this marriage needs to end ASAP

I imagined you
needing to read every single phrase
over and over
put a big X in every box

I wished badly
that legal documents

could hold you accountable
for giving up on us.

I wished
your signature meant
owning your shortsighted, impulsive decision
instead of agreeing with a catch-all
legal jargon
bullshit
cop-out statement like
"Irreconcilable Differences."

I bet the lawyers that came up with that phrase are the same kind of asshole you are.

Diana Medina

Dearest Ex-Husband

I hope you have deep, chronic, painful ingrown toenails
to keep you company
on every step you take
in your new life
without me.

I hope you get ringworm.
The literal embodiment
of the kind of person you are:
a mold like parasite.

I hope your dog takes a shit on your pillow every morning
to remind you of what you brought to my life.
I hope you get heartburn
with an intensity equal to the amount of fire
I had for you that burned without question.
I hope you cut a jalapeño
then touch your eyes and scratch your balls.
I hope your baby momma takes your entire paycheck for child support.
I hope your belly grows so big you never see your dick again.

I hope your Wi-Fi
works at a slow glacial pace and
buffers constantly until your last breath.

I hope all these things for you because discomfort is a prerequisite to growth.
As you move through life with your fragile ego in the driver seat
I'll be here
rooting for the universe
to bless you with discomfort.

We were together long enough for me to know
I'll be drinking the day I find out you've died.
I am not sure yet if it will be in sadness or celebration.
Either way, it would mean I have outlived you.
Until that day, or the day that my rage converts to indifference,
all I can do is have hopes for you.

InstaChivalry

You said "I want to grow old with you"
but in the time we were together
my life grew mold from you,
my heart grew cold with you,
You couldn't ever do what you were supposed to do,
You were all words and empty promises never any follow through.

So skilled at spinning chivalrous tales for the gram
collecting likes and comments as if that was proof I needed
to know that you were always good to me

Constantly saying "but look how the world sees me?"
Behind closed doors I felt different and knew better
You were too distracted
collecting like after like
Believing the bullshit of your fabricated hype
never giving me what I needed when no one was watching

There is no time to snap a picture
when you're being a rock for someone
when you are putting that person before anything or anyone
when you are doing the work you signed up for when we said "I do"

It was for better or for worse
not for likes on the gram
Now that I know who I am
I see who you are
A shell of a man, all ego, fucked up
Like Pavlov's dog drooling for that thumps up
Addicted to filtering pictures
to hide the lies you cover up

The fake validation of social media will never be enough
You can't hashtag your way to self-worth
You have to walk that walk
do that work

You pretend you're a nice guy but
your heart is a field full of dead roots
Wisdom won't bloom there and neither will a purpose

Your life on the gram is like a piece of shit covered in glitter
It may look nice and shiny under all those saturated filters
But in the end, just like you, it's a stinky illusion

How to let him go

You will need:
- Black sunglasses
- A Disneyland season pass
- A bad bitch playlist
- Gal pal with the day off and a car

Steps
1. Cry your eyes out
2. Put on black sunglasses
3. Ask gal pal to pick you up
4. Play your bad bitch playlist on the drive to Disneyland
5. Arrive, eat churros, and drink beers (yes today this constitutes "a meal")
6. Ride the TeaCups while screaming "you ain't shit [insert name]!!" until you puke or experience euphoria (whichever comes first).
7. Repeat as needed until catharsis is complete.

Diana Medina

Death at a Brunch

I went to brunch by myself
I sat at the bar watching couples share food.
I thought about the end of our laughter
and all the things that remind me of you.
I wondered if there would ever be a day when
I no longer think of you at brunch
or when I see caramelized shallots,
or smell freshly smoked bacon.
Probably
but it wouldn't be this day.

The server brought me a coffee
with the most adorable itty bitty milk jug
like a tiny 1950s milk gallon
a side of nostalgia with hipster flair.
I reached for my phone to call you,
catching myself before I fell too far into the past.
I wonder who I could call now to laugh
about this adorably, ridiculous milk jug?

No one would say "it's mini!" in a high-pitched voice
and listen to me rave on and on about how I found
yet another small thing that makes me feel like a giant
when I hold it in the palm of my hands.
No one but the you I used to know...
The you who, in this moment, haunts me
with the scent of memories in my food
and the sounds of your voice dancing around me.

I started drinking alcohol
hoping it would erase you from this meal.
My drunken tears brought me a new conclusion:
I wasn't just having brunch alone today
I was also the only person in attendance
at the funeral of an inside joke I will never tell again.

Green

I dress myself in green, the color of life
I make myself go out into the world
though I feel lifeless and sad inside
I do what I can to muster up a smile
I take a selfie to post on Instagram
filtering my pain with clarendon optimism
partially for the world but mostly for me

I take one last look in the mirror
This dress covers the places
where he used to touch me ages ago
when I liked it
when he still tried
when I didn't know
anything better existed

I have been doing this with dance trial and error
Attempting to abandon my pain at the bottom of a drink
Trying get over him by getting under someone else
Telling myself that this was all for the best
hoping one day that phrase will be louder than my hurt
But pain doesn't understand perspective
It just feels what it wants and picks at itself

I wonder what I did that made him go
trying to pinpoint the exact moment
Was it when I asked him to love me harder
because I couldn't find the strength to love myself?
Was it when I ran out of ways to fake my happiness?
Was it that hard to be around me?

Maybe it was my light that scared him
Maybe it was too bright for him to witness every day
Maybe my light started giving his ego a sunburn
I suppose no one with thin, fragile skin like his
can handle being married to a rising sun.

IKEA

Why do people hate IKEA?

When I come here and watch couples arguing over bedding and cabinets
I see a commitment to marital bliss when the honeymoon phase fades.
I see 2 people caring loudly in opposing directions about their home together.
Is that not what it looks like in practice to build a life together?

One partner committed to a color scheme
One partner committed to utility
Both partners so committed to each other
that they will endure long lines and mazes
while participating in a series of negotiations
that will ultimately end in one of them building something
that will hang or sit in a home in a suburb somewhere
collecting dust as it fades into the background of their life.

I see couples lost together in the warehouse section
trying to figure out if they need boxes 1 and 2
or 3 and 6 for their dresser or bed
I see men who are more committed to their woman and their home
than my ex-husband was to me and ours

This is the underbelly of marriage
It is not glamorous or filtered for the 'gram
where its participants are invited to take a stand
and understand the needs of their partner
while staying the course together
despite how much they piss each other off
because the only way to get out of this Swedish godforsaken place
is to go forward together grabbing what they came here for
so they never have to come back again.

Some people would call that work but isn't it just love in another form?

Dead Weight

Someone once told me
you were the weight to my balloon
I thought that meant you kept me grounded

In reality that meant you kept me stuck
tethered to a place where I did not belong
chained to a life of limits

Free to roam with you
but only within the borders your fears defined
unable to do what balloons are meant to do

Your grip on me was the reason why
I could always float but I could never fly

Rare

The love I gave you was rare
unconditional,
all encompassing,
illuminating

A day will come
when you will need it
and no longer have it

You will search frantically
in the spaces all around you
until you find someone
that feels close enough.

You will think you've won
until you notice how their love
only illuminates new kinds of darkness
coming through all the me-shaped holes
you slowly and mindlessly punctured
into all the things you wish were different now

Acceptance

One day it will come just like a sun comes every morning

    Acceptance

Acceptance that...
    ...life is better
    ...a chapter of wasted time can yield wisdom
    ...living your best life is state of mind, not a competition
    ...sometimes your new life will have to coexist with old pains

On those days, starting again is the most radical act of courage you can choose.

Painful Mantra

Every day for the last year
I have woken up telling myself:
what was no longer is

Some days that mantra is motivation
an invitation to jump into newness
something joyous that I celebrate

Other days that mantra is met with dread
tears blur the blessings I'm surrounded by
as I am overcome by a deep sense of loss

On those days, I am a mess and somehow
I will myself to go through the motions of my life
forcing myself to hide my mess behind a smile

One day soon when I tell myself that mantra
I will be filled with peace instead of sadness
maybe I will even cry when I say it

On that day when I look around in tears
I will clearly see what has grown anew
and be grateful to my hands for what I built

Maybe that will be the day I feel normal again

Good Hair Day

Today feels heavy
Too heavy for me to face
Too heavy for me to pretend I am ok

I force myself to get dressed
I make myself put on shoes
I order myself to eat breakfast
because a heart full of emotions
shouldn't feel on an empty stomach

On my way out I see my messy hair
How it has the audacity to look lovely
On a day when I feel like crap

Unbeknownst to me
my hair decides to confront this day
by protecting brain and adorning my head
with a crown of effortless waves
the perfect look to sport
as I reign over today's sadness

For that act of resistance alone
It deserves to blow in the wind
Even if the rest of me is still crying

Reinvention

First there was the hard fall.
The one that reminded me nothing is forever
And left me new bruises and scars

Then there were the feelings
The ones that turned my eyes into rivers
The ones that turned my heart into a crime scene

Then there were the reunions with the parts of me that I lost
The ones that the mirrors in my life forced me to remember
The ones that show me how the new me and the old me coexist

Then there were the friends
The ones that gave me the strength to peel myself off the couch
The ones that brought me back to life

Cover Up

You may see me smiling
but please don't be fooled.
Every now and then,
there are battles I fight
with no one but myself.
In my mind's war zones
over time I learned the art
of smiling at my friends
while fighting my demons.

Healing with crazy glue

Healing is like watching someone pull out every single emotion you are capable of feeling, lay them out on a table, and randomly start smashing them with a sledge hammer.

You have no control over what shatters and what doesn't. All you can do is pick a corner of the table and start gluing your broken emotions back together while others are still breaking.

You can't do anything about it or save everything. You have to think like a project manager when all the tasks are behind or the president when he has to pick which place to bomb. You have to prioritize.

You have to look around at the shit show and ask yourself: What can I do right now with what's in front of me? Which part of this table will give me the most bang for my buck? Then just pick a spot and just start gluing while you can still hear the banging and breaking in the background.

Eventually, you get a groove going with the glue. Then you pick up another piece to glue but realize there is nothing to glue it to. You are now at a new part of the table; unchartered territory of broken shit that you haven't ever seen before. You realize that little thing you just picked up belongs to a bigger thing you haven't dealt with yet and now you can't keep gluing.

That moment when you are standing at the border between the state of pain and the state of growth is microscopic in the healing process. It sneaks up on you suddenly. One minute you are thriving - making a little girl's day because you saw her magic and made her feel understood, feeling accomplished at work, feeling desired by someone you like, walking home enjoying the trees because you finally taught yourself how to breathe, and then you see it: a trigger from the spare piece of the thing you haven't dealt with staring you in the face.

Your flow stops because you've crossed a state line into a new part of your table. Before you can continue, before you can ask yourself those questions about this moment... you are in shambles, frozen, unable to see beyond this broken moment. You forget about your day. You forget about your progress. You forget about all the good shit.

In your head, your feelings are in a town hall meeting and its public comment time. The coalition of grief, gloom, and sadness have the floor and you have to listen. That moment lasts the longest not because of time but because of pain and you have to have it before you can keep gluing yourself back together.

So Feel

The only way out of hard feelings is to go through them.
Embrace solitude, fall apart, and remember:

Feeling our feelings is what reminds us we are alive.
Feeling our feelings is what reminds us our hearts still work.
Feeling our feelings is what confirms we have a stake in our life.

So feel
Feel all of them
Treat them like a guest in your home.
Embrace all of what they want to tell you.
Wisdom will emerge from your pain.
Joy will emerge from your wisdom.

So feel
Feel painfully.
Feel epically.
Feel beautifully.
Feel the hurt.
Feel the regret.
Feel the memories.

Let your heart grieve what could have been and wasn't
Let those thoughts turn your tears into fuel.
Tears are holy water of your own making.
Holy water that has power.

It cleans souls.
It washes wounds.
It clears emotional debris.
Let that water flow out of your eyes and into the world.

Your tears are showing up to wipe off
the beautiful canvas that is your face.
After this you will be prepared to light up again
to witness and find joy in all that is on the horizon.

So feel

Do Over

Today I hit refresh
On this moment
On this day
On this life
Emotional buffering complete
A new page opens
and I take my first step
into a different story
where I am both villain and hero
and I fight myself to save myself

Diana Medina

Getting Back Up

After the fall, things feel dark,
bleak, painful, and scary
like nothing will ever be right again

Your home is a cluttered mess
that looks like a giant came
picked it up and shook it
turning everything upside down

Suppressed emotions spill
from eyes and mouth
from boxes in closets
from a heart that can no longer be strong

Nothing is where it should be
your attempts to put things away
and get it together feel pointless
All you can do is cry
All you can do is forget to breathe
All you can do is think thoughts that make no sense

Then you hear it
the sound of your tribe catching you
Loving you through your pain
even when they don't know how

Family Requests

Stop
Stop worrying about me
Stop treating me like I am dumb and helpless
Stop turning my darkness into your crisis

Consider
Consider that you prepared me for these battles
Consider that my faith is strong
Consider that my heart is evolving

Remember
Remember who I am
Remember that I am a piece of the best parts of you
Remember that you taught me strength

Start
Start cheering me on
Start trusting my instincts the way you trust yours
Start treating me like a piece of yourself

A tale of 4 tattoos

1 - The hummingbird is the only bird that can move like a helicopter. It flaps its wings in a figure 8 as it hovers around gardens drinking shot after shot of nectar to quench its thirst. It can even fly backwards but won't. Dude, that life sounds pretty sweet.

2 - La Virgen de Guadalupe had a crescent moon at her feet, didn't she? I think maybe I do, too. Sometimes, I am not sure if its waxing or waning though. Why not both?

3 - If you take your first step into a new chapter with love, a community will appear. Even if you get lost.

4 - When you plant a sunflower on the sternum it grows like a weed. It is the only way to protect the heart from breaking again. It's like having a beautiful botanical bodyguard. Her weapon of choice? Fe.

5 - I always said I'd never love anything enough to get it tattooed on my body, not myself, not him, not my family.

6 - Tragedies, dark times, and clowns have a way of changing how you feel about such things.

7 - If you choose your birthmark wisely, every tragedy becomes a rebirth, darkness turns to light, and clowns leave your garden alone.

8 - My mom said "que vergüenza" when she saw them. Verguenza means shame and according to her I don't have anymore. She's right.

Apartment 8

Since I moved here, I have laughed a ton
I have lost my mind and found it at least 3 times
I have contemplated infinity and what the future holds for me
But I was today years old when I realized
I was in this exact room the day I found out what he did
The day the fear I said out loud in a moment of vulnerability
became real live, hot off the presses text messages from little birds
with tattle tale claws sending me modern day ravens
they were seasoned with a bitter mix of screenshots,
unfiltered bluntness, and unsolicited chisme commentary
The news and his posted words hit the back of my throat
like cayenne pepper going down my windpipe

I coughed until I started to cry
I cried until I started to laugh
I laughed until I started to cry again
I cried until I fell asleep
That version of me was devastated.
I laid there quietly wondering
if I am in fact powerful enough
to make any fear I say out loud
become a real live Instagram dagger
or if I am just a melodramatic idiota
who gave her best years to a turd.
Looking back now, I think it was both
and maybe a bunch of other stuff, too

I was in this room when it was not my home
It was a living room with a different couch in it,
facing a different wall, home to a different person
a friend who lent me her a sympathetic ear,
and got me the interview I had the next day.
I don't remember what happened from then to now
I don't remember how I got the job
or how I moved in to this apartment months later

Diana Medina

I just know I sat among boxes for months
meticulously turning my pain into home decor
using a color scheme to declare
it's my house and I live here now
I don't know when I decided that
each time I walk into this room
I wanted to feel this box shaped sanctuary
lovingly slap me in the face then kiss me on the cheek
as it says "pendeja!!! where the fuck have you been?
Come sit down. We missed you!"
My refuge could not be dim or bland
it needed to be bright like the days ahead
I don't remember how in the world
I packed all this stuff to bring here
But I remember every place and lesson
that led to me acquiring each treasure

A crappy brown painting of a vase
The first thing I haggled at a flea market
I framed it to put my negotiation skills on display
A piece of art I got as a gift
from my first internship after college
A woman with a flower in her hair
Looking off to the side surrounded by sun
A pink patchwork footstool I saw on a sidewalk
one day after I spent too much money on brunch
I saw it and felt a stirring in my gut so strong
I picked it up, carried it in the store and
bought it without asking how much it cost
It didn't matter. I loved it that much
and for the first time in my life,
I had the money to spend on just me
One of many micro-moments
of post-divorce liberation
There is no one I have to run this by
It's MY house and I live here

My home style is something
my best friend calls "super ugly"
for its unapologetic use
of every color that makes me happy
Purple - the mixture of red and blue,
blood and tears, rage and calm
Teal - like the ocean, like the perfect mix
of blue and green, of sea and tree
Yellow like the sun, rising again, glowing
like light bulbs full of new ideas
Gold like the thing I am worth more than
Black and white like the type of communication
I expect when my heart is involved
Grey for the times that doesn't happen

This home is a style that proudly declares
"The woman who lives here
will not live a life surrounded
by beige and bullshit.
This woman will walk
on this colorful ass rug
the way Jesus walked on water
and be a whole ass vibe.
This woman will live a life
surrounded by meaning,
moderately priced midcentury furniture,
and shit her Apa built custom for his baby."

I don't know how I didn't see the way before
My taste, my choices in rugs, my teal sofa,
My purple table, my bright yellow dresser
are all a rebellious response to the moment
I found out that news and spent the night crying
staring at the shape of this room when
I was supposed to be sleeping in it
that night back way before I ever lived here

I remember coughing, crying. laughing,
then crying again, hard
with my whole soul
I have no idea what memories or feelings
were attached to
which tears
or which laughs
But I remember this room
I remember how the front door
only locks from the top
not from the bottom
there's a metaphor for my body
A home with a door
A space I will occupy on my terms
This room went from the scene of a crime
to the poem that I get to live in

Where the fuck is my discipline?

I have gained so much
weight during this pandemic
thanks to being sheltered
in my sedentary ass place

Don't get me wrong
I am thick and I feel sexy
The only reason I want to lose weight
is because it is the cheapest way to
to fit back into all those cute clothes
I have collecting dust in my closet
I don't want to buy shit all over again

Maybe it will get me to stop
wearing nothing but yoga pants
Maybe it can cure my depression
Maybe it can calm my anxiety
It would be so nice to give
those stubborn twosome shit to do
'cause when they pair up
they run amok in my life
tag teaming on travesuras
that do nothing but fuck my day up
making my brain feel so heavy
and my heart feel so bare

All I can do is drown in my tears as I
struggle to catch my breath on my couch
The problem is that the only one
who can whip them into shape
at the same time is my discipline
but when the pandemic hit
my discipline was on vacation
(she accrues 2 days per moon cycle)

She left Soledad in charge while

she got stuck somewhere tropical
where the sand is at her doorstep
and the air smells like salt and possibility
She's not in a hurry to come back to work
she's been tanning, reading, swimming, and
having a fling with a hot waiter who works
at the all-inclusive resort where she is staying

I called her ass and told her
I needed her
I need her to get out from under that waiter
I need her to get her ass on a flight
I need her to be here Monday morning at 9am sharp
we got work to do, shit to manifest, and pants to fit into

Motherhood, Womanhood, and Me

I have to say the thing
The thing that is hard to say out loud
The thing that is hard to put in writing
I am struggling...

Struggling to see my peers become parents and grow their families
Struggling to live in the era of pregnancy photo shoots
gender reveal parties, birth announcements, monthly baby pics
Struggling to hold space for my friends who are tired parents
Struggling to hear the women in my life cry and say the things
they are afraid to say out loud
about their children, their spouses,
about marriage, about motherhood, about adulting
The thing I am afraid to say out loud:
I don't think I want children

Don't get me wrong
I love other people's kids
I love my nieces and nephews
I am even nurturing as fuck
But I don't think I desire motherhood
or the exhaustion that comes with it
I am struggling with that feeling
this is not something a Latina says out loud
In my familia, in my cultura
motherhood IS womanhood

I remember the countless times at family events
birthday parties, baptisms, and baby showers
How I'd make my rounds of saludos and
the senoras would put their hands on my belly
And say "y donde estan tus babies, mija?
I would smile, take their hand off me, and keep going
deeper into the party and taking more of the same bullets.
The entire time I wondered,
when did I agree to meet this expectation?

when did I consent to my womb being community issue?
when the innate desire to have children didn't overpower me
I thought something was wrong with me
I ignored my inner struggles and just gave in
to my mother who would constantly say to me
"No me puedo morir sin tener uno de tus hijos en mis brazos"
To my husband at the time who had been collecting
sporty baby clothes since the day after we got married
I never agreed to have them
I just agreed to stop trying NOT to
We tried to get me pregnant for 3 years
Sex stopped being for pleasure, it was only for procreation
The whole time I worked to wrap my brain around this idea
Motherhood... me as a mother, my partner as a father, us as a family

Eventually I got pregnant and a whole set of new bullets came
The unbearable pain and bleeding I had at work
The fear I had about losing my job with a culture so toxic
that I worked a whole 12 hour day with that pain
Going to see the doctor the next day and getting more bad news
Being told the baby got stuck in one of my scarred fallopian tubes
The doctor telling me I had an untreated STI that caused the scarring
Me looking at my husband, the only person I had slept with in 13 years
Him yelling at me in the car after the appointment saying
"How dare you accuse me of causing this" before I even said a word

The rest of the months' long ordeal is a blur
The deep sadness and feeling of incompleteness I felt
The anger with god for making this happen to me
The indifference from my partner
The many, many, many comments from woman saying
"It's ok you can try again" or telling me how many times they lost babies
The follow up appointment with an insensitive doctor
The moment I was told it was not safe for me to have babies without IVF
The moment my husband, the person I loved most, asked me for a divorce
The moment 2 months later when I found out his new girlfriend was

expecting his child
After all of it, I wondered if this was god's way of telling me motherhood is not for me

I wondered other things too
I wondered if it was payback for all the times I had premarital sex
I wondered if it was payback for my choice to marry a man and then raise him
I wondered if it was payback for taking birth control
I wondered if it was payback for smoking too much weed in college
I wondered if it was payback for other sins I can't remember
Most of all, I wondered if it was payback for not sticking to my own guns in the first place

When people ask me if I want to have children now
I still don't know what to say...I am leaning towards no
Motherhood seems beautiful and transformational
But the painful journey I have gone through was too
A child free life where I get to be the cool tia has other benefits
A life where I get to have freedom from the expectations of others
A life where I get to break with traditions that never served me
A life where I get to travel and see the world and build a different legacy
A life where I get to be a meaningful part in the upbringing of children around me
A life where I get to finally, finally, finally worry about my needs and no one else's
That kind of life was never available to my mother, or her mother, or her mother
That kind of life sounds pretty amazing
It's not wrong to want that life... is it?

Airbnb

It was my first time in New York
My first vacation alone
the most meaningful, irresponsible
financial decision I ever made
I will never forget it

I arrived early to my airbnb
A grey building with no elevator
It had old with copper mailboxes
black and white checkered tiles
I carried my bags up 5 flights of stairs

The door opened before I knocked
out spilled a girl in tears holding a purse
Our apologies bumped into each other
like bumper cars at a clumsy carnival
eventually we parked in her living room

She was giving me the tour of the place
holding back tears in a way that was familiar
I gently interrupted her coffee machine tutorial
to tell her it was ok if she needed a moment
She stopped what she was doing to burst

Her shoulders releasing heaviness as she said
"My boyfriend broke up with me yesterday"
Damn and here I was three hours early
trying to stay in this woman's house
as her freshly broken heart was falling apart

I told her she looked the way I looked
the morning I showed up to work
after my ex asked me for a divorce
within hours after the shock still trying
to function instead of feel… I've been there.

On that day, all I wanted was a pause button
I offered her a seat on the daybed across from me
she sat on the floor with her purse in her hands
as if this was only going to take a minute
I held space for her as she put it down to feel in front of me

Some while later she finished checking me in and we hugged
I thank her and told her it was an honor to stay in her home
In the week I stayed there, I blessed that space for both of us
with Palo Santo, prayers, poetry, pot, and a Puerto Rican lover.
This would never happen at a Hilton or a Marriott.

Diana Medina

Los Lyfts del Norte

In the hour drive from my
Airbnb in Long Island City
to my flight at La Guardia,
Juan made every effort
to ensure I felt welcome
and comfortable in his vehicle

The customer service went out the window
once he heard me speak Spanish
He said he was Dominican and pulled over
Our accents danced around each other
like long lost family catching up

He invited me to sit in the front seat
We bonded over our mutual love of
Los Tigres Del Norte and Banda El Recodo
I sang "La Puerta Negra" with this man
I only do that with close friends and family

He told me about his life in New York
I told him about my life in L.A.
Both our stories got the full telenovela treatment
followed by heaping servings of advice from our
Mamas, Abuelas, and Tias on these matters

We took breaks between conversations
to loudly sing the lyrics we loved
along with the songs playing on the radio
We said dios te bendiga to each other
when we got to the airport

I suppose all of that plus the fact that
he had plenty of gum, water, and
hand sanitizer in the vehicle would merit 5 stars.

Last Male Friend

You used to run into the middle of
long lines at amusement parks,
discreetly hide yourself in the crowd,
jump high into the air,
and then wiggle your body.
From far away it looked like you were a dolphin
jumping out of water waves made of people
Every time you did it, I laughed until my abs hurt
But I struggle to write about you

You crossed a country to see me
then out of nowhere you crossed a line
Maybe you figured "I came all this way
what's another couple of steps?"
You never told me how many drinks it took
for you to ignore me when I said no.
You were a main character in my personal Wonder Years
Now you are the reason I don't have male friends
I'd never want to be a few drinks away from being a victim again

But I went to your funeral anyway...
Before you taught me what sexual assault was
you taught me how to run without losing my breath.
You helped me conquer my teenage angst
one fear and insecurity at a time
You were there when I rode my first roller coaster
You there when I smoked my first joint
You are the reason I randomly quote
Wu Tang Klan and Busta Rhymes
The way people on IG quote Oprah
or Warren Buffet, or the bible...
Around you, every radio playing hip hop
became a church with a motivational speaker

When I run into people with your name
I wonder if that is you sending me messages
When I hear Wu Tang on the radio
I wonder if that is you trying to talk to me.
Sometimes when I remember you
I see pieces of me I am trying to get back

And I struggle to write about you
I struggle to accept what you did
I don't know how to forgive the unforgivable
So I just love you and hate you at the same time
both sides will always grieve for you

Block

I had to do it.
It hurt so much.
I didn't want to.
I really didn't want to.

There was part of me that had hope
We could somehow stay connected
Maybe timing would be better
Maybe all this love I had for you
could covert itself to friendship overtime

My heart is not wired to take on
friendships with former lovers
Especially the kind who only seek me out
for free therapy and ego boosts

So, I deleted you, your name, your photo
I blocked your number from my phone
I put up every single cyber barrier
I could think of to keep my fingers from finding you
It was the right thing to do

And now I miss you.
I miss touching your skin.
I miss the pieces of friend that were in you.
I miss laughing from a deep, real place with you.
I miss how time use to stop when we sat together on my sofa.
I miss the way you'd bring me McFlurry's when I was having a hard day.
I miss the way you'd bump my shoulders with yours when I'd say
something wise.

Most of all I miss you when my back itches in that place
between my shoulders that I can't reach on my own.
You always gave the best scratches in that spot.

When he comes back

First, he will text you out of the blue
You fall for the idea you can be friends
But he is simply priming you for access
And since you are still not over him
you reply but not like you used to
You use less words and emojis
Keep your excitement to yourself

He makes up a reason to be near your place
He will ask if he could come by "just to say hi"
You make your first mistake a second time
when you let him in and greet him with a hug
You think "at least I didn't change or dress up"
He sits on your sofa right in his old spot
It took you months to get his scent out of it

Then he will sit right next to you feigning concern
He is just checking to see if you're good
Before he unloads all the reasons he is not
You will listen and your eyes will tear up
because in that moment you will catch yourself
doing it again... loving this person who hurt you
You struggle to resist the urge to save him

Then he will look you in the eyes searching
for validation, for an ego boost, for an opening
something to show him he can still wiggle back in
still get access to you without earning it

This is how the boy exploits
unsuspecting soft spots in a woman's heart
with eye contact and fake concern

Spa-bservations

Everything is beige here
There is vanilla in this free tea
I ain't mad at it. It's pretty good.
There are also free cookies
The cookies are also beige
I had 6 of them
There is a fruit bowl next to the cookies
I grab a banana and 2 oranges
after scarfing them down
I realized two things
1 - I didn't have breakfast
2 - I am pretty sure the fruit was a decoration
because my stomach is still grumbling
and the fruit bowl display now looks lopsided
the only thing keeping my grumbles a secret
is the harp music playing in the background
I have no idea where it's coming from
perhaps the beige section of heaven?

I am wearing a white fleece robe
the only thing I've seen so far that isn't beige
it is so soft and it has a hood
Seeing all these people wearing them
makes me feel like I joined a relaxation cult
I wonder if anyone would notice if I stole it?
I think the towel lady can read my mind
because now she's following me
maybe she knows I want the robe
that's one person who would notice

My masseuse is a tiny petite woman
she walks me down a beige labyrinth
of halls and doors into a room
there are more harps playing
I disrobe and lay on the table
I hear the voice of my mother inside my head

Diana Medina

She's freaking out about how naked I am
"Andas con las nalgas al la intemperie!
Que el señor te reprenda!"
I laugh at it like a small act of rebellion
the massage begins
And just when I start questioning
if I'm even going to feel anything
from this tiny lady's tiny hands
she starts going in on my back
smoothing out my lumpy muscles
pressing on the stress I've been hoarding
Work stress, Life stress, Love stress
my house is a mess stress

I wonder what chip is still on my shoulder
When she starts using her elbows on me
My bones are cracking and crunching
like a delicious deep-fried tortilla
and at that moment one thing is clear -
there are enough chips on my shoulders
to make a whole platter of nachos
out of the burdens I have yet to release
She starts kneading me like I am like a piece of tough dough
As she is pulling and pushing and pressing
I think: this must be what it feels like to be silly putty

Rosario

"Todos los días rezamos un rosario por ti"
My mother reminds me of this every time we talk
I hated praying the rosary as a kid
The repetition, the chants, the songs
The prayers in Spanish that I memorized but never understood
I recited them along with everyone else like a robot
Faith never felt right to me this way
So structured and inflexible
I remember the feeling of the rosario beads between my fingers
I would hold them and follow along
The señoras would look at me and say
"Mira que bonita te ves resando mija!"
They didn't know I was just counting the minutes 'til it was over
If I didn't follow along it would feel like an eternity

My parents find comfort in this type of prayer
But I don't, I find it limiting, uninspired, suffocating
As I think this thought, mother also reminds me
"Todos los días primero rezamos un rosario para ti
y luego rezamos uno para los demás."
How should I take these words from my mother?
I am the youngest of 8 children
I have 22 nieces and nephews
and I get my own daily rosary?
My parents pray for me first, then pray for everyone else
I wonder if this because I am the biggest sinner,
the biggest failure, or the biggest disappointment?

As a kid, that morsel of truth would have won me
every fight I ever had with my siblings
No matter what they did to me or how they tormented me
this would be the mother of all comebacks
While watching TV, if my brother would change the channel
I could say "Whatever... our parents pray for me first!"
Or when my sister would take my toys from me
"You can have that toy. I get my very own DAILY rosary...

you have to share yours with everyone else! Like a peasant."
I imagine myself a small, petulant, unibrowed child
Being openly grossed out at the thought of my blessings touching theirs
That would have been such a comfort

I ask my mother why?
Why do you pray so much for me?
"Es que nos preocupa tu situación. Andas por todos lados.
No encuentras tu lugar. Queremos que te calmes."
I have never been freer
and my parents think I am lost
I have never been happier
and my parents are worried
I tell her this but it doesn't matter
they will still worry about me
The baby of the family
no husband, no children,
all alone in the big world

I say what I say every time we have this conversation
"Amá… ¿dónde está su fe? ¿Cuál es el punto de preocuparse
por lo que ya puso en las manos de dios?"
When we say a prayer isn't the point to
give it to god and not take it back?
Her response is always the same "Es que tú no eres madre."

I wish there was a world where my way of life
inspired pride instead of worry in my mother's voice.
A world where I wouldn't have to remind her about faith
"Es que me preocupo mucho por ti! Estás lejos! Estás sola!"
In the absence of a man, my mother found worry to take his place.
It is precisely because of that abundance of parental protection
that I ventured off into the world to plant roots in a new place.
Why waste all those prayers on a one block radius?

I don't know if it's an honor
to be prayed for first
To be protected first
or to be worried about the most
What I do know is that
this conversation is one of many
where I have to walk my mother towards
rethinking her worry
Rethinking tradition,
rethinking what it means
to have a good life

Rather than argue with her again I simply say this:
"Gracias. Las oraciones de los padres son las más poderosas
Esa protección diaria es un divino guardaespaldas para mí.
Tal vez, por eso que siempre ando con la rienda suelta
Sin poder encontrar mi lugar porque gracias a esas oraciones
El mundo es mi lugar. Mi corazón es mi lugar
Mi pasos están guiados por algo más grande."
Her response is always "Ay Diana, tú no me entiendes.
No hay quien te gane cuando se te mete una idea a la cabeza"
My response back is always "Y por eso se que voy a estar bien."

Diana Medina

Cry Me a Narwhal

No...
Don't.
Don't cry me a river.

Cry me a swamp
Cry me Niagara Falls
Cry me a narwhal
Cry me a humpback whale
Cry me a coral reef
Cry me a shark
Cry me a penguin
Cry me a mermaid
Cry me a dolphin
Cry me a duck
Cry me a loch ness monster
Cry me a continent
Cry me 100 oceans

Cry me every undersea being
and ecosystem imaginable
until your tear ducts rupture
and your face becomes
what your heart always was:
an empty, desolate, polluted,
purposeless, lifeless wasteland.

While you're at it
cry yourself a ship to sink with
be the captain of your own Titanic.

My lifeboat set sail for safer arms,
clearer waters, greener pastures,
and better love eons ago
with no desire to return
to the cage you call a life.

Inner Child

My inner child is still pissed off
about my brother scaring me
the day before my first day of kindergarten.

He told me the teacher would shoot me
if I didn't know the pledge of allegiance by heart.
He said the teachers carried guns in their fanny packs.
He took me aside to "help me practice"
When English words felt too heavy for my tongue,
he pulled out his pretend finger gun and said "boom!"
I believed him.

On my first day of school, I was so terrified.
I tried to escape and got stuck in a hole in the fence.
I cried when they got me out of it.
The teachers got me unstuck and walked me into the classroom.
I sat on the carpet shaking
thinking I'd be dead soon.

A little boy named Charlie sat next to me.
He held my hand as I cried.
He kept saying "don't worry. I am with you."

Adult me tells my inner child it's ok.
I say, "Adrian didn't know what he was talking about.
Look, we didn't die. We have 2 degrees now."
I agree to play Tetris with her while eating Lucky Charms later.
Unlike my parents, adult me can afford to buy her
all the sugary breakfast cereals she wants.

Go Get It

My guides came to see me today.
They interrupted my depressed comatose daze
The way paparazzi surprise famous people outside the gym.
They were decked out in the strength of my heritage.
walking in front of me striking poses like starlets at Oscars.

Their hands felt like cool wind on my cheeks.
They dried my tears and moved my hair off my face
They told me truths about me that I struggle to hold on to
when times are hard and my heart is lonely.

They said:
You are not lost.
You are not a disgrace.
You have come home to yourself
after being away for a lifetime.
You are not locked out.
The key to enter the temple that is you
has been in your pocket this whole time.
You have looked into your soul's eyes and saw a galaxy staring back.
Your soul never runs from you
even when you run from it.
Your power
makes souls that haven't met themselves
pee their pants.

Don't you remember planting flowers in your garden next to your flaws?
They are bright and bloom through every single pore on your skin.
Don't you remember holding hands with your beauty and listening to her sing?
Her melody is embedded so deep in your bones it fuels the way you walk.

Don't you remember how you gave your inner child
the clothes off your back and told her she was safe?
You grabbed her little hand, you apologized to her, and whispered:
"Mija, you deserve the world. I am going to go get it for you."

That is a commitment that cannot be unheard or unsaid.
And while your past cannot be undone, unseen, or unfelt,
your future from this moment forward is yours for the taking,
Yours for the molding, yours for the moving, yours for the changing.
So, get your ass off that puddle of stagnant quicksand
you call a couch, put on some pants, and go get it.
She is waiting and deep down inside so is the rest you.

Inner Teenager

My inner teenager feels restless about all the unknown we are walking through.
She is pacing all over the house trying to come up with a plan to fix every worry.

She paces anxiously blurting out fragments of a master plan saying:
"This is how we will start a business.
This is how we will get a new job.
This is how we will find a new man.
This is how we will lose weight.
This is how we will read 100 books.
This is how we will get 3 more degrees."
She is making adult me very anxious.

She always took matters into her own hands.
When my parents told her she was too young to work
she snuck out and got herself a job anyway.
When my mom told her she was not supposed to do that
she said, "Nimodo. Empiezo la semana que entra."
She even forged my dad's signature on the work permit.
It was easy, they both do their M's the same way.
My mom lectured and yelled at her but had no choice but to accept it.
My dad was angry at her for the forgery but he admired her.
Her decisiveness, her work ethic, and resourcefulness made him say:
"Ay mija, te pareces tanto a mi."

Adult me tells my inner teenager that it's ok.
Yes, we are both upset about having gained so much weight.
Yes, we are both worried about not having a job.
But we've been able to live in leggings and bra free for 6 months.
Let's not ruin the sweet liberation for our boobs today
just because we don't know what will happen tomorrow.

Breaking up with a compass

He said he was tired of listening to her
He said he was tired of wandering through trees
He didn't like where she said north was
That direction looked too steep, too challenging
He said he would be better off on his own
Asserting he'd get to his destination faster
and have more fun without her weighing him down

The compass delicately held silence
Watching the man spin in circles as he left
Alternating between thinking and tripping
Walking in one direction then another then another
His feet unable to find steps that felt like conviction
How was that better than knowing where to go?

She felt sad as she thought of all the dust particles
that would eventually accumulate on her face
She felt sad to have been discarded by the man
She had grown so attached to guiding him
She felt like an extension of his palm and fingers
What would she do now alone lost among the grass?

Diana Medina

What is Love?

I don't think I know anymore
I have broken my own heart
1,000 times
trying find the answer

Searching for it
in indecisive arms
giving it generously
to liars and leeches

Finally finding it in my puppy's eyes
She looks up at me beaming
full of unconditional admiration
grateful for any bit of acknowledgement

This is how I must have looked
to those idiots I tried to love
like a tiny lost puppy orbiting them
waiting for scraps of affection

I looked at them as if they were
the last drink of water in the desert
the last taco on my plate
the cheesy dust at the bottom of the Cheeto bag

I made them the center of a universe
I never bothered to properly explore myself
My world was ok
as long as our skin touched
so I gave and waited
and gave and waited

Healing Out Loud

What did I get in return for that devotion?
I got really good at being a doormat
I got really good at looking the other way
I got really good at thinking I deserved them

Maybe love is just me in my car
with a kick ass playlist on an open road
and my pup watching me cycle through
cries, screams, and smiles until I feel free

My Religion

My religion is
Kindness, Authenticity, Love
Something the recognizes the pieces of god in you
because it finally sees the pieces of god living in me

My religion is
Joy, Hilarity, Comedy
Something that laughs with its whole heart
Because the creator has a sense of humor

My religion is
Freedom, Purpose, Hope
Something that rebels against containers and structures
because dogma and salvation aren't one size fits all

Stockpile of Grace

The work of deep inner healing requires
patience, foresight, understanding, grace
There will be days when it all makes sense

Days when your purpose is clear
Days when you feel yourself healing in real time
Days when your wounds turn into wisdom before your eyes
Days when the pains you've endured finally start to fuel
the inner strength your heart has been thirsting for

Be present those days
Have gratitude for your journey
Stockpile all the grace you possibly can
Later there will be days that are a fog

Days when new realizations are sprinkled in among old memories
Days when triggers flood your new life
with painful reminders of things you thought you'd forgotten
of outdated versions of yourself
Days when your will impulses choose your path,
not your heart, not your wisdom, not your higher self
Days when you feel yourself going back
into the same war zone where you got these wounds to begin with
Days when the pain of yesterday is back, hurting, and vengeful
stomping all over the healing you've built like Godzilla destroying a major city

On those days you'll be glad
you set aside that stockpile of grace
to remind yourself you are worth it
to help you forgive yourself

Sola

Como un frijol en olla grande
Como el último pedazo de carne en la parrilla
Como una tortilla dura
Esperando en paz
Hasta que alguien me haga taco.

5 Year Old Swag

How amazing would it be if we all lived life
with the swag, certainty, and fearlessness of a 5-year-old?
That is the age when the world had not yet told us
we couldn't be our full, rambunctious, and confident selves.
The age when imagination, creativity, curiosity, and wonder
spilled out of our being with fervor and authenticity.
The age when the word "why" was an invitation
to make meaning out of norms, traditions, people, and life.
The age of dreaming out loud, discovery, scabby knees,
dirty hands, and playful disobedience.
I will be going back to that place starting today.
Join me.
It'll be fun.

The Noise

Search for the noise
the one whose rhythm
dominates heart beats and
the dancing of souls
Jump and fly
You are armed with wise smiles
and protected by the strength of your ancestors
Go forward without fear
Leave your shame behind
Let the vibration of your breath
guide your steps at every moment
Listen and feel inside
YOU are the noise
The ears of the world
are hungry to hear you

Go Get It

My guides came to see me today.
They woke me up from my daze.
Decked out in the strength of my heritage.
I saw my light in the pupils of their eyes.
Their hands felt like cool wind on my cheeks.
They dried my tears and moved my hair off my face
They told me these truths about me and my journey:
There is no such thing as settling anymore.
You are not lost.
You have come home to yourself after being away for a lifetime.
You are not locked out.
The key to enter the temple, that is you, has been in your pocket this whole time.
You have looked into your soul's eyes and saw a galaxy staring back.
Your soul never runs from you even when you run from it.
Your celestial magic makes souls that haven't met themselves run from your gaze yet seek out your energy.
You have planted flowers in your garden right next to your flaws.
They are bright and bloom through every single pore on your skin.
You have held hands with your beauty and listened to her sing.
Her melody is embedded so deep in your bones it fuels the way you walk.
You gave your inner child the clothes off your back and told her she was safe.
You grabbed her hand, apologized to her, earned her trust, and then whispered:
"Mija, you deserve the world, so let's go get it for you"
That is a commitment that cannot be unheard or unsaid.
And while your past cannot be undone, unseen, or unfelt
Your future from this moment forward is yours for the taking,
Yours for the molding, yours for the moving, yours for the changing.
So get off that puddle of quicksand you call a couch and go get it.
She is waiting and deep down inside so is the rest you.

The Armpit Apocalypse

I have a theory that God is in cahoots with my mother.
Together they are plotting to help me see the light.
I know this because today God showed up to my job
and dropped a tiny bomb in the middle of my work meeting.
I was facilitating a conversation and raised my hand to point at something.
In that moment, I realized that I forgot to put on deodorant

The sweat I collected after walking in the summer heat was performing an unwelcome, olfactory symphony for my nostrils and the ones of those around me.
I remembered in that moment how my mother had talked to me about reading the bible more because we are in the end of times, and she wants to make sure I will be saved when the end of the world comes.
This apocalypse of funk coming out of my armpits gave me so much anxiety it felt like the end of world
And as I smelled myself, I could hear her words and feel my stink making me more and more self-conscious by the minute.

I know the word apocalypse means the revealing of divine mysteries, and in this moment, the most divine mystery of all was the aromatic armpit Armageddon that was interrupting my meeting, ruining my confidence, calling into question my credibility as a functional adult, and making the attention spans of all my colleagues dwindle as they wondered, "What the hell is that funky smell" - that moment was a revelation.
And I thought, isn't that also the name of the book in the bible that talks about the end of the world?

I think that is the book we were talking about when I was in my confirmation class as a teenager and got kicked out for asking too many questions about God's intentions.
It made the teacher uncomfortable that I wanted to discuss her claims, and she told my mother
My mother was so embarrassed that I didn't just listen. "Ay que vergüenza" she said, embarrassed by my display of curiosity and critical thinking.

I wondered then the same thing I wonder now about faith and religion: Am I supposed to feel so stifled in God's house?
Doesn't God want me to ask questions?
Isn't that why God gave me a brain with the ability to reason?
Doesn't God use my day to day life to send me signs of things I need to know or be aware of?

And if that is the case then isn't it plausible that this attack of armpit funk is the end of the world for me? My anxiety and shame seem to agree.
Perhaps this is how God is teaching me about the Book of Revelations at my mother's request.
Putting embarrassment into a context I actually understand - what a revelation.
The main things this revealed to me:
1) Deodorant is a lie masking your true scent to the world - so be suspicious of people who smell too good to be true, and when your funk comes to the party, just own your truth.
2) Getting ready when I'm in a hurry makes me forgetful - so be present and vigilant and every moment and sniff the pits before leaving the house. You don't want your truth sneaking up when people aren't ready to know it intimately.

And, most importantly 3) In order to be ready for an apocalypse of any kind, just keep a travel size deodorant in your purse, car, or desk to prevent the proliferation of future unwanted funk until the time is right to reveal the smell of your truth.

Staying Unstoppable

How does one stay unstoppable when everyone and everything is trying to test me, distract me, control me, and stop me?

Can I just live? Can I do this my way? This meaning - my healing, my job, my career, my life, my outfit, my hair...

I don't need you to come tell me what I already know
What I need is for you to understand why I know it in the first place.

I know it because I listen. I listen to my heart, to my soul, to my body, to the wind, to the mountains, to the trees, to the moonlight.

Do you have any idea how much you can transform your life when you just listen and pay attention?

I listen and the wisdom seeps into my body through my cells and into my bones.
It fuels the direction of my inner compass when clutter and noise don't let me see the way.
They encompass every part of me.

My toes wiggle when I hear wisdom making the earth shift beneath my feet.
When I smell the wet earth after a storm, I hear the songs of my ancestors affirming my strength, affirming my resilience, affirming my resourcefulness, affirming ME.

When the skin on my face feels the wind, it's like getting butterfly kisses from God.
They are filled with tenderness, protection, ease, and guidance.

If you could only see how clear things are for me, you would understand what I now understand:
That I am destined to be blessed.
That I am fully prepared to walk through shit to get to my paradise.
That God, the universe, the spirits of mis abuelitos, my ancestors, the moon, and every other life force out there has my back.

They guide me. They love me.
They move me to my purpose.
So, stop asking me questions about my stuff.
Just follow my lead and deal with yours.
They want to guide you too, and I don't have time to stop

Four Walls

To my body these four walls were a haven
The first place that was all mine
These four walls were my safe space
On this floor, I fell apart on my terms
On this floor, I put myself back together
On this floor, I cried many tears
Tears of sadness, pain, pleasure, and joy
This is where I learned to truly exhale

To my soul these four walls were a battlefield
The site where I fought daily with my demons
Where I called myself on my own bullshit
Where I learned to not be afraid of my myself
Where I unlearned things that weren't serving me
Where I gave words to the voice and fire inside me
Where I began to embrace my essence

To my future self these four walls were a classroom
The place where I learned the sound of peace
The place where my solitude became sacred
The place where I welcomed others into my orbit
The place where I finally came home to myself
The place where every lesson was a springboard
To greener pastures and better days

Titanic

A friend sent me a quote this morning that said:
"Live life like the captain of a sinking ship."
I was like: How?!?!?!
Locked in a room drunk wondering where it all went wrong?!?!
I saw Titanic.
I remember that scene where the captain drank his scotch and contemplated his mistakes before going down with the ship.
Honestly, I don't think I could go out like that.
At least not today.
Today, I woke up in a dark mood.
Today, I would be the kind of captain that would deck all the women and children in my way and take a lifeboat for myself.
Why the hell not?
Closed mouths don't get fed and drowning ones don't get to live.
And I want to live, but I just don't want to go to work today.
So I pull my hair back and put on my armor of hoop earrings and red lipstick and come into the office.
Really I just want to stay home and contemplate all the apocalypses my friends keep posting about like their horrible bosses, stupid people who don't know how to park, or the latest presidential tweet.
I think I won't survive any of them just because I haven't watched the news, been to the gym,
or written a poem in over a week.
This darkness is a new feeling for me.
I usually find a way to be joyful.
Some would say I am terminally whimsical
But today I just don't have it.
My wise friend reminds me that, "it be like that sometimes"
Maybe I don't need to go to the gym or watch the news to survive an apocalypse .
Maybe I just need a pink gat, a blunt metal object, a bedazzled crossbow, my words on these pages, civic engagement, and the desire to not go out like that drunken chump of a captain on the Titanic, whose final moments tasted like regret and failure.
Armed with those things, perhaps I'm good.

Labels

Don't dismiss my scars as baggage
There is no better way to know me
than to learn how I was torn apart
and understand what parts of me
I slowly bartered away in exchange
for snake oil disguised as love

If you trace the seams on my soul
with curious fingers you will see
the many places where I reattached
the remnants of me I was able to recover
among the ruins of my pains and failures

You'll notice how I reconstructed a spine out of bones and branches
borrowed from my ancestors and how I made a garment out of all the
red flags I ignored in him to shield me from the cold he left me in and all
the haphazard patches I added to fill in the many holes left behind by the
parts of me I lost forever
Or all the tiny burn marks on my fingers that I obtained from painstakingly
attaching words to the fire inside me with a hot glue gun to make myself a
new voice

That is the reason why I am mine before I am anyone else's
This process of putting me back together
with seams and patches and burns is my life's work

In the moments when I feel most alone, feel most vulnerable, feel most
defeated
I remember what it took to get myself back
I remember how hard I am working to make myself whole even if that
process makes me look like a mismatched quilt

Because at the end of the day
I am most myself when I fall apart
most myself when I feel all that requires feeling,

all that is too much
all that is too intense

I learned long ago that to feel and to fall apart is to know you are alive
To fall apart is to know where you stand and what your boundaries are
To feel is to be free and exercise choice in paths, potential, and perspective
To be free is to let your emotions breathe without restriction
and I have drowned them too many times before...
my emotions need oxygen
I need to know them
see them,
meet them,
hold their hands,
look in their eyes,
and ask them what they need from me

Asking those questions is how I found out
that my anger needs space
my anxiety needs grace
my hope needs affirmation
my pain needs a hug
I will not walk a life where I am blind to myself
if that means I am labeled intense,
labeled too much,
labeled annoying,
labeled crazy,
labeled extra
Then I have to wonder who decides labels to begin with?
Who is the most important designator of the labels of this world?

I closed my eyes as I contemplated that question and immediately an image came to mind of The Creator walking through this world holding a label maker, only the world is just an Office Depot warehouse and all of us are sitting in plastic storage containers...
And The Creator's fingers are methodically typing out divine designations and categories for all of us on the tiny buttons. Then the creator hits print

and smiles as that delightful little strip comes out
I hold out my arm for my label but
The Creator sticks it on to my forehead Instead

I catch a glimpse of my reflection in The Creator's eyes before I blink, and I see it
I see 1 word, 5 letters, the label that overrides all the labels I've ever been given
W-H-O-L-E. Whole.

A vision of Home

Be ready
Flow
Reach
Your inner compass knows the way
Surrender
You are whole
You are enough
From this day forward
rooted in the sweetness of your life
you will bathe and swim in honey
Slather the building blocks of your new life with it
Your destiny will stick to it
Rise as both queen and worker
maker and creator of your magnificent hive
Laugh for it
Reach for it
Breathe for it
Discover life in color
You will be pleased with it
Brown and blue like soil and sea
Grey and green like sky and tree
Your life will be a garden
blooming flowers and bearing fruit
years of labor will be rewarded
Rising like suns and mountains
You will shine, mija, you will shine
The life you built will be a work of art
So live loud and be free powerful woman
You are home.

Mundane Blessings

It's Saturday, 3:08 PM
No one's looking for me
No one asked me how I slept
No one needed me to dress them
No one said good morning
No one made me coffee

I think, "I should be productive today"
I remembered I hadn't paid my rent
I attempt to go pay it, but my car won't start
I've been meaning to get that fixed
A change of course
I put on my tennis shoes and call a Lyft
I drop off my rent check and walk home
I need a haircut
I watched videos on YouTube on how to cut your own hair
I didn't trust myself enough to do it
Odd, the things we trust strangers with
I see a Supercuts, the stylist has purple hair
She senses my trepidation and only cuts off an inch
I ask her to wash my hair because I don't want to do it later
I can afford to pay for this convenience today
I check my phone again
No one is looking for me

The cost of my good life

In response to: "Stop being sad and just be grateful."

Just being grateful is not that simple
Yes, it has been scientifically proven to rewire your brain
Yes, gratitude is powerful
but it's one of the hardest muscles to work out in the middle of a shit show
It's not an eraser that overrides other emotions
You can be grateful about one thing and grieve another
You can be grateful about one thing and cry over another
You can be grateful for one thing and feel sad about something else entirely
You can be grateful for all the things and still be hurting inside

Gratitude doesn't just erase pain
Gratitude doesn't fast forward healing
It is not that simple just like a good life is not that simple
That is why gratitude is a practice, not simply a feeling

And maybe my life wouldn't sound so good
if you knew what it cost me
If I showed you all it's taking me to remodel it
I have been a one-woman crew on a construction site that is my life
Have had my heart broken and foundation cracked
More times than I care to count
Getting your heart broken and your foundation cracked that many times
is the emotional equivalent to losing everything in a hurricane

Precious things get damage beyond repair
And though most of the things can be replaced
What made them precious is gone forever
and there is no FEMA to help you rebuild after that level of loss
You have to file that claim directly with god
And the piles of divine paperwork associated
with filing a claim for that level of emotional damage

is always painful, messy, unpleasant, unclear, bureaucratic
and completely lacking in good customer service

That's the thing about people
we always covet the things others have
but we never ask about what it cost them
And if by chance we come to know what the price was
we snark and say "well never mind that's too expensive"
as if wisdom or freedom or awakenings
are readily available on a clearance rack
And we wouldn't be caught dead getting those thing unless they go on sale
God forbid we pay full price for life experience

Alone

I look for peace in my silence
Searching for stillness in a moving city
Desperate for space to let my thoughts breathe
and allow emotions once consuming me to speak
Anger says, "I am pissed off"
Grief responds, "I know"
Sadness says, "I am hurting"
Hope responds, "It'll go away"

Glow Up

I walk under the cover of darkness
Exposing my skin to the night sky
Hoping light from the moon and stars
Plants into my pores and eyes and hair
I want to wear this cosmic glow in daytime
Someone should compete with the sun tomorrow
Why shouldn't that someone be me?

Go On

be the crazy tia
say the things that no one does
challenge antiquated ideals
move to that new city for opportunities
wear that dress and black sheep badge
with pride and fierce, fiery freedom
drink that drink, smoke that joint
laugh when you're happy
cry when you're sad
show off your mess and your magic
sing that song loud as fuck
make a dance floor in the sala
call your loved ones on their shit
smile at those strangers' judgements
tell the world you're not alone, you're free
move towards things that heal you
your sobrinos are watching you
show them there's another way to live

Open Ears

I listen to the trees, to the wind, to the moonlight
Their wisdom seeps into my body through my cells
It cuddles lovingly with my bones until they exhale
My heart and soul take in all this divine coding
They use it to fuel the direction of my inner compass
and then when clutter and noise don't let me see the way
my toes wiggle and I hear wisdom making the earth shift
I smell the wet earth after a storm and it awakens me
I hear the songs of my ancestors affirming my strength,
affirming my resilience, affirming my resourcefulness, affirming me
And then my face feels the wind like butterfly kisses from god
Filling me with a sense of protection, ease, and guidance.
All of it reminding me that I am fully equipped and prepared
to walk through shit and challenges to get to my paradise
because I am destined to be blessed.
The only thing in my way is me.

Greñuda

The hairs on top of my head
are a reflection of my insides
Messy and all over the place
Screaming so I don't have to
I am awake and alive this way
I could tame them and myself
But the truth is I don't want to
All this freedom feels too good

A Date with Fire

The first time I met fire it was so bright.
I didn't think I would ever see it again.
I couldn't help myself. I wanted to go towards it.
I ran to it full force knowing the contact would hurt.
I knew I was going to burn all over.
I knew I was going to have all the scars.
I thought, since I will never see it again
I will only have to do it once. Just this once.
I thought, if there is some wisdom that only comes
from pain then why not move through it?
Why not let fire touch me, burn me, and scar my skin?
So I can say I did it and have the bravery to prove it.
So I can touch it in my hands and know how it feels.
So I can watch myself heal before my own eyes.
What better way to witness the full range of my humanity?
I did it with a combination of fear and excitement.
I met with fire face to face. I shook fire's hand.
I kissed it, I danced with it, I let it burn me over and over.
When fire left, I was in pain and awe contemplating all I got
from the experience and from the aftermath.
I missed fire so much I decided to go meet it again
Because this kind of healing feels too beautiful
Now I don't know any other way to heal.

An Act of Revolution

Con la música en alto
I set my body free
Unafraid and uninhibited
I feel all the love I was made with
as my hips sway and breasts shimmy
My pain surrenders to the thoughts of self-love
that I buried deep inside my bones
no longer hiding them from myself
I express all the feelings of gratitude that
my curves have been longing to hear from me
Finally feeling caresses from my own hands
My limbs excited to be witnessed
My lips saying DAMN at the sight of me
In all my glorious movement
My heart feeling butterflies
at all the essence of me I am serving
at my soul's sexy smile
Por fin getting a look at all of me
My skin takes a breath and sighs
Soy bella y mi cuerpo lo sabe

Con la música en alto
I allow my hands to greet my curves
My hips and legs and arms rejoice
They hold space for my chakras
to move, meneando sin miedo
My shoulders and face move together
in magical unison like protective pillars
framing my yoni's liberation dance
In certainty and sabiduria
in the power of my abuelitas
in the guidance of the moon
rooting me, holding me, healing me
I inhale passion and exhale doubt

The fire inside me pulls back the curtain
to let this magical creature be seen
by the parts of me that feared her
and as we dance I can finally breathe
We embrace and I become whole
My higher self takes a breath and whispers
Soy magia y mi cuerpo lo sabe

Cafecito

It wakes me when I arise with a warmth that coats my throat in the sounds of Amá, Apá, Abuelitos, and tíos having conversations where volume is irrelevant, and the earth stands still.
Sharing stories of other times, better times, times from the rancho, times of their youth late into the night.
Oral history weaved into hilarity with equal parts wisdom and belly laughs. Every sip covering my tongue in the taste of humble hospitality at the end of family parties where each cup shared creates connections as the pan dulce flows freely and abundantly.
The smell of it awakening my childhood memories of dipping galletitas de animal into my cup letting them go and watching them swim in circles.
Brown cookies float in brown cafecito with just enough milk to make it look like my skin and just enough sugar to remind me of the sweetness of life.
Drinking it is like looking in a mirror and seeing my roots staring back.

Who I am

I laugh loudly with my whole body
I feel all my feelings very deeply
Intensity and emotions flow through me like a rip-tide
From the top of my head to the tip of my toes, all of me feels
I have the world's worst poker face
My joy and sadness are always present on my face at the same time
My feelings are a symphony the world sees in the pupils of my eyes
I talk with my hands at all times. I can't help it.
My fingers are desperate to be part of the conversations of my heart
Words that convey feelings this deep need epic, animated emphasis
When I dance, 80% of my moves are in my face
My body is just following my spirit's lead
The broken parts of me dance as beautifully and joyfully as the happy parts of me.
Both of them merge together in my face, my hands, and my body like a perfectly imperfect mosaic of wounds, wisdom, heartbreaks, memories, and jokes.
Not everyone has what it takes to love, like, or even befriend an intensely badass, deep-feeling, open-hearted, determined woman with boundaries and kick ass dance moves.
I have accepted that my magic is not for everyone.

Experiencia Religiosa

When times get tough and
you don't know what to do
just masturbate
and then
go to church.
You will find answers
in one or the other.
And if not
At least you'll have an orgasm

Diana Medina

Anatomy of a spark

South LA 2001
A college party held at someone's friend's mom's house
Loud music blares in the backyard
The front porch looks like it puked people
onto itself and the front lawn and sidewalk
She makes her way in anxious about her curfew
He comes in later not sure what he is doing there

Candy Rain plays and only two people sing along
Without coordination, they take turns singing the verses
Their eyes and body language immediately on the same page
Both of them sing confidently but also loud and very off key
With terrible pitch on the "Candy coated raindrops" part
They don't care. The whole room laughs at them.
When the song ends they introduce themselves

Three hours later the duo is still standing in the same spot
A whole cycle of festivities transpires around them
Drunken coeds orbit them like planets around the sun
Two by two just like in Noah's Arc only the arc is just a party in a house with no AC
Their eyes, smiles, and jokes building onto each other
Like perfectly proportioned toppings on a subway sandwich
Their conversation moves at a rate of one lifetime per minute

They start dancing together
First "Motown Philly" by Boyz 2 Men
They go parallel, far apart, choreographed
like boy bands, back up dancers, or big bangs
Running man, kid-n-play, cabbage patch
they do all the OG dance moves
they follow the commands of beats and rhythms
good little soldiers in a dance party army
Eventually "Tempted to Touch" by Rupee
The go face to face, close together, touching
They are like peanut butter on jelly,

hummus on cracker, stripper on pole
Touching, grinding bodies, grazing skin
Moving together in unspoken synchronization
Exchanging laughs and whispering in ears
Until her curfew comes or his ride leaves
Whichever comes first

Fuckboys and Ice Cream

Do you know what I saw when I first saw you, Fuckboy?
I saw sex in a pair of jeans, a smile that made me feel warm and gooey
and a full head of hair that my fingers wanted to swim in
You, Fuckboy, looked like the kind of fuck I needed after the heartbreak I had
The kind of fuck that would treat me on the outside
the way I was treating myself on the inside:
Tortured, bruised, and indifferent to my pain
Too hurt to see my gifts
Too scared to hear my words
Avoiding eye contact and my invites for deep conversations
The kind of fuck that would punish my ego
the way I was punishing my heart for loving and losing
Being with you was like eating ice cream
Always delicious in the moment
Every flavor dancing on my taste buds
Sweet and tart and complex
Everything an ice cream moment should be
Then I learn the same hard truth about you that I know about ice cream:
The flavor only lasts a moment
It's always gone too soon
I'm always left thirsty afterwards
And the part that stays behind feels icky on my skin.
Yet I let you in my house and in my bed
Because I want ice cream when I am sad
Because I want company when I am lonely
Because the only way to overpower the flavor of my tears
is with the comfort of something overly sweet and overly tart
Something that tastes so good has to be bad for me
Something that makes me look for permanent peace in temporary pleasure
Always hoping for different but just getting more of the same

Call of Booty

When you walk towards me
there are no words
Everything is feeling
A sexy heaviness hanging
in the silence between us
Eyes close and mouths open
Face to face and skin to skin
We rock together slowly
until we lose control
I let go when you hold on tighter
My moans get louder when you get quieter
As we both get closer to where we want to be
I release and you stop
Slowing your cadence
My body follows your lead
You admire what I spilled for you
You fill your bag as I continue to empty mine
Out of breath and spent, we admire what was collected between us

Company

You weren't a great love or lover.
Not even close.
But you were company and
Having company was better than being alone
when the hurt in my heart was too much to bear.
Having company was better than being alone
when I wasn't ready to deal with my own truths.
Having company was better than being alone
when it was so much easier to soothe the brokenness in you for a night
than to soothe the brokenness in myself for the rest of my life.
If that's a task that will take me a lifetime, can you blame me for
procrastinating, getting that started by saying yes so to having a little
company over?

Because you know what I was taught to do for company?
I was taught to treat their presence like an urgency that must be handled immediately
An urgent task to replace the real work of the day
As a child, I remember how my mother would stressfully yell
"Viene visita!" "Company is coming!"
That was our cue to respond to this fabricated crisis
We'd drop all the shit that was happening in our day to day life
We'd clean the house or just shove our mess into a closet so it looked clean.
We'd shower and put on our "nice" clothes
even though that is never what we'd actually wear at home
We were trained to only speak in only pleasantries
To be good hosts and defer always to the needs of our company
even when our whole world was falling apart.
Because "We don't make a scene in front of la visita"

So I did that for you because it's what I learned to do
I put on my best face even when it pained me
I put on my nice clothes when all I wanted to do was stay in that soft comfy pair of sweats that had a hole in the crotch and an enchilada sauce stain on one leg

I put a smile on my lips when all I really wanted to do was scream
"Can't you see that I am barely holding on?"

Years of indoctrination on the ways to deal with company means
I was well versed in the art of swallowing my inner turmoil
like bitter cough syrup with a smile and projecting a "no trouble at all" vibe
I played host to you while I was lifeless inside
I offered you water, food, and shelter
I served you the pieces of myself that I was saving for a soulmate
I brought them out, like fine china and expensive wine, for you because you were company
And I was taught to do anything to make company feel at home
even if it meant sacrificing my own comfort, my own heart, my own healing.

Back then I always found myself asking,
Why do we go through all this trouble for someone who isn't planning on staying very long?
Last night after you left, I wondered the same thing.

Lost and Found

I mistakenly thought you might belong to me
because I found you in my bed that night
But I had to learn the hard way that
when people are lost and end up in your bed
they don't want to belong to you or anyone else
They are just running from their healing
looking for a convenient place to crash
after they had too many drinks
and you didn't have enough boundaries

To my hot neighbor

I first laid eyes on you when I was moving a box into my place.
I ran into you in the tiny hallway between our two doors.
You were in a hurry and avoided my gaze
But that will not do for me sir
As a member of the Mr. Roger's Neighborhood generation...
I know how to be a good neighbor.
So I blocked your path and said, "Hi! I'm your new neighbor"
I smiled and extended my hand
You said, "Hi" as we shook
My fingertips grazed you softly as they lingered on your palm
My skin wanted to milk every drop possible out of this neighborly touch.
I said, "How are you doing?"
You said, "Good. I'm always good."
I said, "Of course you are" as I looked you up and down
I wanted to say soooooo many other things:
I wanted to say "Damn."
I wanted to say "I heard you and your girlfriend last night... I think I can do you better"
I wanted to say "Has anyone ever told you that you look like Cinnamon Drake?"
I wanted   to say "Big, buff, bearded? You might as well be kryptonite."
I wanted to say "Your cinnamony hue looks like it would mix well with my cafe con leche skin"
I wanted to say "You're what Mexicans call a "Taco de Ojo" - a taco for the eyes
And do you know what you and tacos have in common? You're both the perfect 2 AM snack..."
But I didn't.
We just met.
I just moved in.
That would be weird.
So, I just let the silence hang between us
I let you feel the weight of my stare
I noted how the hallway we share is small enough for me to smell your scent.

I made a mental note to take a whiff of you the next time I "accidentally run into you" on purpose or the next time I "don't know how to use the dryer" and need some help
Until then, your purpose will be emerging from apartment 7 for my visual delight.
Like a sexy buff and bearded cinnamon sunrise,
what a beautiful new day it will be...

The Precipice

I'm teetering
walking the precipice
between running from you
or leaping towards you

Some days I can picture it
Me opening up all I am to you
in hopes that you will greet me with open arms
But most days I just keep you at arms distance to prevent your potential rejection
Some days, I want to let myself feel all my heart thinks about feeling when you touch me

Most days, I recite the same mantras in my mind
"We are not building, we are passing the time"
"It's normal to mistake warmth for feelings when it's cold and someone holds you"
"Don't feel first, don't fall first,
it will hurt, he will hurt you"

I hope it keeps my feet on the ground
and my tears in my eyes
so you won't see them
and I won't feel them

But despite my best efforts
I definitely feel them
So, you probably see them
and instead of talking about them
they just hang there between us
not helping the situation but
not getting in the way of it either

Keeping us warm but in limbo
not able to end it and not wanting to take it
to a more meaningful or defined place
Sitting on the precipice together
between what could be a great love
and what is probably just a random winter fling

Blinded by potential

I can't say that I loved you. I didn't.
I just knew that I could love you if you let me.
But I did like you. I liked you so much.
So much, I settled for a mediocre friendship
and endured the pain of my hurting heart
just to be in your company a little bit longer
So much, I let your indifference empty me
until all I could see was the ugly side of you,
the stupid side of me, and one painful path to clarity.

Industrial Dick

He's got a heart of gold
and an industrial dick
He is like a steel beam
breaking all my buttresses
tearing down all my walls
He builds monuments to my moans
in all my vaginal jurisdictions
Like a titan of industry breaking ground
all over my body all at once
Carefully constructing warehouses
to store the chills, shivers, and shakes
he extracts from each section of me.
Executing elaborate strategies for my divine demolition over and over.
Who needs to rebuild when falling apart is this much fun?

Love letter from an introvert:

For you, my darling
I would leave my house to endure unimaginable tortures...
like leaving my house
like crowds
or tourist attractions
or long lines
or Sunday brunch
or IKEA
I would smile for pictures
I would dance in front of you
I would make small talk with strangers
If we were lost, I would even ask for directions
I would gladly face all my fears as long as I could do it in your company

To the hot farmer dude at the Midtown farmers market:

The crowds parted and then
I saw you standing at your booth
a stunning, brown, agricultural Adonis
in your natural habitat
Strong, scruffy, strapping,
I thought your parents must have made you
with extra love and passion and sweat
because dammmmmm....
saying you are easy on the eyes
would be the understatement of the century
You were wearing a baseball cap
and jeans and t-shirt were tight yet loose
the right fit to show me that you
could probably bench press me...
I stood still admiring you...
all bronze skin, big lips, and broad shoulders
It was as if god herself went down
into the vault in my vagina
where I store my deepest desires,
pulled you out of my fantasies,
and placed you in my path today
and I don't like vegetables
but for you that could change...
I was mesmerized by the way
your hands were touching the melons
cupping them firmly and gently
as you showed a group of customers
the best way to select one to purchase
I had no idea fingers could have biceps
As you talked, I pictured those buff fingers
grazing my shoulders after a hard days work
There's probably remnants of soil under your fingernails
I'd enjoy the smell of earth on your skin
and the caress of your calloused hands against my body

I imagined it would feel like getting a massage from a burlap sack
a little scratchy, a little soft, a little rugged, a little rough
just the way I like my rubdowns...
You looked at me with your deep, dark, brown eyes
they were like pools of chocolate pudding I could swim in
and you said, "May I help you ma'am"
Your deep voice made my ovaries tremble...
and I was fixated on the movement of your lips
pressing together when you said may and ma'am
my full lips excited at the idea of them
mimicking the moans we might give each other
Your mouth would be a worthy opponent
during a steamy make out session
Together we could make first base great again
Then in that moment I realize 2 things:
1) I am very obviously eye fucking you and
2) I was woefully unprepared for this grocery
shopping trip to be such an erotic experience
BUT I am already here, I have gone too far into this booth,
and I have looked at you too long to turn back now
Plus, I am not one to waste an opportunity
to make a memorable first impression
and this romance has to start somewhere
even if that somewhere is just me purchasing
the fruit and the veggies that have had the good fortune
of being touched by your beautiful muscular manly hands
So, I take a deep breath and gather all my courage
I stand up straight, I smile, I adjust my hair
Then I look you up and down and up again
and when your eyes finally meet mine I say
"Yes, tell me about your zucchini..."

Marky Mark

I was 8 years old when the Good Vibrations video came out.
It is what confirmed to me that I was straight.
Watching him dance and work out shirtless
made me feel so warm I thought I had to pee.
Years later, when my fingers discovered we could feel that good vibration
any time we wanted it was the best day and longest shower of my life.
I have been feeling the vibration and sweet sensations ever since.

Dollar Tree Spooky

The character Spooky from On My Block can get it. The cholos in my high school didn't look like him. If they did, my heart would have more bullet wounds and teardrop tattoos than I could count.
I dated a dude once who looked like a knock off
version of Spooky you could buy at Dollar Tree.
He drove a burgundy Buick with a grey, velvety interior and a bumping stereo system.
When we went on our first date he got out of the car and knocked on the door even though I told him to just honk. He said, "Nah, I'm a gentleman"
He said hello to my father with altar boy deference. They shook hands for a really long time. I was surprised when my dad still let me go.
My dad was always a good reader of people's character and intentions. I guess he knew that there were some cholitos
who have hearts and skeletons and kindness hidden under those barb wire facades they call attitudes just like everybody else.
This guy wasn't Spooky hot, but he was handsome. He definitely knew how to treat a girl.
We never had sex, but I once covered his entire back in hickeys while he told me all his secrets in the back seat of his car.

Winston Duke

He is what I would classify as a chocolate lumberjack
Big, black, beared, bronzy, and thicc....
On dating apps, the ones who look like him always get me in trouble. They are my kryptonite.
And since I have no shame or control
I have no problem telling them so.
At first, they like it and think it's funny.
Then they think my confession gives the upper hand.
What they don't know is I tell them that for my own sake not theirs.
If it ultimately goes nowhere, as most of these interactions do, I can feel proud that I survived a battle of wits with my biggest weakness.
And, in the rare times it might turn into more, I can forgive myself for
not being strong enough to resist when it ultimately blows up in my face.
Superman's issue with kryptonite was always about his own demons not the villain's.
In the movies, when he was around it, he'd be weakened but still put up the best fight he could.
Around these chocolate lumberjacks, I am the same way.
Most of these men run as soon as they find out my shit is more elevated than their childish flirtation games.
I do not compromise any sides of me.
I am a freak but still a lady.
I feel hard, fuck hard, and love hard because how does one go if not hard?
This sounds like a great deal until they realize I am interested in fucking more than just a body.
They got to come build some cabins at the top of the mountain between my ears that is my mind before they chop down the forest in my pants.
I still haven't met one who is fearless enough to make such a climb in real life.

Spank Bank

A man in every color has had me,
wronged me, and slept on my greatness.
Each of them was just like me;
A little bit ancestor and oppressor rolled into one.
I could break ancestral patterns and heal oppressive traumas in my bedroom
with any one of them for hours on end.
Skin to skin on my kitchen floor, we'd develop delicious recipes to take back stolen lands, break each other's chains, and rewrite our histories.
They'd thoroughly enjoy the way we'd smash the patriarchy, dismantle systemic oppression,
and build new pipelines to sexual consciousness.
When was the last time your orgasm came with a side of liberation? For me, it was last night as I loved myself to sleep. For these beautiful famous men, who knows? For the shortsighted men who walked away from me... never.
My bedroom and my body are the historic sites of la reconquista, la guerra de los sexos,
la liberación de mis demonios simultaneously.
I believe in making love that focuses on mutual liberation. It is sensual, intelligent, witty, and in the words of the great modern day She-losopher, Cardi B, "litty like a motherfucking titty."
I keep the lights on to not miss a moment of the transformation and witness the litty in real time.
So, if I ever get such an opportunity with any of these muses - celebrity or civilian - trust that
I will be sure to put my back and being into it. When it goes down in my imagination I always do.

Soul Mate Job Posting

I am currently accepting applications for candidates to participate in a real live committed, monogamous transformational love affair in the physical world with me. Candidates must be on a first name basis with their soul, pass a verbal exam, clear an extensive background check, and participate in a series of interviews with my higher self and spirit guides for consideration.

Addendum: This is a highly selective, highly competitive process. The most prestigious love in the world should be.

Fat Shamed

I was fat shamed for the first time on a dating app today.
Some dude who messaged me seemed nice until it was evident what he wanted. I made a commitment to myself to hold out for quality interactions, not hookups.
So, I didn't respond.
He was buff and attractive in his photos, but he was not bringing any conversation of substance to the table.
So, I didn't respond.
He messaged and messaged saying we could smoke, that we could blaze and chill
saying, "let me know sexy."
I didn't respond and then the comment came:
"I guess not. I hope you are working hard to lose that excessive weight."
I didn't respond. I blocked and I reflected.
I reflected on the notion that a man with such a fragile ego, a man that is not of quality would resort to that kind of comment only after not getting the kind of answer he wanted.
I thought to myself, sure I am curvy. Some would say fat. But fat can be lost. An ugly personality is forever - that man and all the men like him on these apps are never going to be able to shed that.
What's more I know who I am.
It will take more than a petty comment from a fragile man-child to break me.
I am a curvy tan goddess.
A man like him, even with his muscles and six pack, cannot handle all this meat and magic.
He's not hungry enough to eat what I am serving.

Temple

People say the body is a temple
I had never felt like a temple before
until he bent the knee at the altar between my thighs
He looked into the eyes of my clitoral soul
He used my gaze as a compass to guide him on a journey
through the disenfranchised territories of my body
He shook hands with every one of my traumas and
planted seeds of safety in each of their gardens
so new things could bloom among the hurt
while a harvest of goosebumps sprouted on my skin
He whispered holy verses into me and worshiped every part of me
until kisses turned into prayers and moans turned into songs
that only me, him, and god will ever know the words to
I will never not feel like a temple again....

Will you hold me?

It's that question...
That moment of complete vulnerability.
That primal need to be touched.
That makes it hard to let you go.
We always asked each other that question
with words and facial expressions.
We obliged one another's request so much
it was hard to tell if what we had was real
or just skin searching for a safe place.
Both are so hard to find these days.

Tears

Tears are a divine gift
holy water of your making
Your body's way of saying
"This matters to me"

Stop hiding them
Embrace them
Collect them
Share them

Baptize your face
as many times as it takes
It's not the worst thing in the world
to know your soul is breathing

What a beautiful gift it is
to turn feelings, fears, and faith
into water and let it flow
out through your eyes

New Vows

dearly beloved self
I have gathered myself here today
In the command center that is my mind
to bring my analytical side
and my intuitive side together
in the ultimate spiritual matrimony
after years of being at odds
both sides finally found themselves
deeply in love and need of one another
in appreciation for each other's gifts
they decided to merge for one joint purpose:
my evolution, rebirth, and growth

Am I there yet?

After years of walking through path after path of dense dark forest
just before I was beginning to question whether or not I am actually loved by god,
I finally saw something that didn't look like an obstacle on the horizon
It was an isolated mountain wearing a crown of clouds off in the distance
Standing there all majestic, high up over the trees and rocks that protects its base   .
A choir of birds with wings extended pass over my head as I admire it.
They are gliding as the wind carries them lovingly towards its peak.
They look patient. Way more patient than I would be on such a flight.
I get frustrated every time god tells me to keep walking towards that peak.
Why can't I just get there already?
Why do you keep sending me on painful detours?
When will I finally be able to arrive, wash the dirt of my dusty pink cheeks, and just relax? I am tired of looking like a hot, brown, crying mess.
Why can't I just get there to see the view those birds are on their way to see?
God smiles at me and lovingly wiping the dirt off my face and says,
"Because my dear, you are not a bird.
This walk is the way you fly."

Good Girl

Teeny, tiny, tan puddle of puppy
hasn't fully grown into her ears
Happily sprawled on the floor
a yellow, unfinished, knit blanket
meant for a baby I never knew
hangs out of her mouth
I tell her it's a hand me down
from her sibling as she chews it up

Out of vergüenza

I don't have any vergüenza left anymore
at some point when shit happens in a life
vergüenza becomes a burden too heavy to carry
Contrary to what cultura and our mothers say
there isn't always honor or pride in vergüenza
Sometimes vergüenza is a survival tactic
Sometimes vergüenza is a trauma response
Sometimes vergüenza is a learned behavior
Sometimes vergüenza is just manipulation disguised
as a request to be quiet, a reminder to stay small,
a command to stop ruffling feathers, or a desperate
plea to please, for the love of god, get embarrassed
The only time I ever hear the phrase "no tienes vergüenza"
was when my individuality, sexuality, freedom,
creativity, politics, or opinions are showing too much
or I dare to take up more space than what is given to me
These things make people and traditions uncomfortable

Messy Roommates

My face flooded with tears today
I couldn't see the floor
or the path before me
or how far I have come
I could only see blurry barriers
I could only feel the heaviness in my heart
I could only hear negative thoughts
Thoughts that sound like my own voice
a voice that is hard on me
a voice that tells me I suck
a voice that doesn't let me sleep
a voice that won't shut up or let me relax
a voice that keeps retelling the stories
of my failures and not my successes
When you are sheltering in place in your own head
it's not easy to be roommates with your burdens
They never clean up after themselves

Conversations with my Anxiety

I wonder about too many things, and then
I ruminate on the things I wonder about, and then,
I start to worry about all the things and what they mean and how they're all broken or breaking and
I can't fix them because there is a whole lot of them and only one of me, and I wouldn't even know where to begin, and I get so overwhelmed I'm paralyzed, and
I start to fear losing control of all the things, and
I want to surrender, but I just don't know how
So, I hold on tighter to all the things even though
holding on to them is slowly killing me, but I figure if
I can't bend the universe to my will, then at least,
I can bend my fingertips around all the things
I can make my grip a little tighter and make my fear a little louder, and
I can worry a little harder and ruminate a little faster and settle into the paralysis...
Some days that small semblance of control is more comforting than surrendering to the unknown

Hoops

I am a force
A vessel of black and brown truth
My presence is resistance
I proudly wear hoops because
I do not jump through them
I might turn down my music
but I will never turn down my energy
My role in the revolution?
To take up space unapologetically
To own my power everywhere I step
You can find me dancing in the fire
moon, mountains, river, and sky
reveling in the majesty
of my liberation in motion
holding, guiding, and loving
every molecule in my being
and every desire in my soul

How to fill your cup

You will need:
* lipstick and/or hoop earrings
* makeup and miscellaneous glam supplies
* a sexy outfit (chonis optional)
* Perreo playlist
* 1 squad of badass mujeres
* sexy dance moves
* a fire pit
* night sky full of stars

Steps:
* Put on lipstick and/or hoop earrings
* Use other makeup and miscellaneous glam supplies as desired
* Put on sexy outfit of your choice (note: sweat pants, rebozos, no chonis, fishnets, lingerie are all acceptable)
* Meet squad of badass mujeres at the fire pit
* Play Perreo playlist as loud as possible (note: be mindful of noise ordinances, perreo party poopers, and such, but do not let that stop you from The Pachanga)
* Do sexy dance moves until you experience mind/body connection, release of power, and/or liberation (note: may take up 15 minutes to reach experience peak intensity; laughter and giggles are sexy and welcome during this process)
* Follow squad of badass mujeres as they dance around the fire (note: when a Selena song plays, divine collective feminine power will be at its peak; Conga lines are most efficient for this)
* Look up at the sky every 3-5 minutes to welcome stars and moon to the party
* Continue with Perreo until inner transformations catalyze, portals open, and souls connect
* Repeat the above steps on own as many times as needed until the light within grows stronger

Have you seen my shit?

It finally happened
I lost my shit
All of it in one swoop
I looked around at my life
My mismatched socks
My cluttered home
My dreams under construction
Everywhere I looked there were piles
of bills yet to be paid
of laundry yet to be done
of demons yet to be silenced
of poems yet to be finished
of hopes yet to be expressed
All of it mixed together
All of it in need of sorting
All of it begging to be organized
And there I was in the middle of it all
Curled up in the fetal position
Crying from the agony of wanting to deal with it
and not knowing where the hell to start
That is the worst feeling in the world

Rejection

It took all of this time to birth this conclusion:
His rejection was not about me at all
I now understand that we both wanted freedom
The only difference was that to me that meant
leaping with him into a future and to him it meant
a space without me, even if it is a prison of his choosing
Our problems always came down to that same fight
A constant battle between follow through and fear
I had all the follow through, and he had all the fear
Love cannot grow in a home or heart filled with fear
That is why it was never going to work between us
Because people with fear run from good opportunities
but people with follow through rise to meet them
And I was never destined to be the queen of a cage

Museum of Me

I put my whole self on display
A sculpture at the museum of me
to admire myself from all angles
I let go of apologies in favor of authenticity
I let go of perfection in favor of passion
I let go of surface in favor of substance
I let go of fear in favor of faith
I let go of judgement in favor of joy

How to live

Dip your toes in your wildest dreams
Feel what it's like to be fearless
Balance on your growing edges
with a tight rope walker's flair
with a daredevil's courage
Let your aspirations transform
Let your heart shine
Let your purpose play
Let it be messy
Let it be mesmerizing
Let it be you

What to wear

Today I will dress myself
from head to toe
In power and purpose
In pain and perspective
In something resembling armor
that can still be playful
In an outfit where I am unafraid
to take up space
to embody love
to fall apart
to hug my fears
to search for peace
to put myself back together
with shakes in my hands
with tears in my eyes
I will say "I've got this"
And I will do the work
To birth a new life

Diana Medina

Niblings

laughs and giggles
from deep down within
wiggles that end
when adventures begin
running on tiptoes
making mischief and messes
living a life grandly
untainted by stresses
with music and dancing
big smiles and bigger screams
and pretty braids and baby hairs
just living and breathing
our ancestors' dream

Dear Poetry

You helped me make sense of my story when it got too painful for me to just live it.
Doing so meant getting access to magic that I didn't know existed.
When you access a certain kind of magic, it always has a price.
I pay your price daily.
I allow you to interrupt me during my day.
I keep a notebook handy to write down the messages you send to my fingers and toes.
I let the people in my life know that they may or may not be an inspiration for content.
I accept that there will be moments when I cannot move or get up or function
until a certain grouping of words are written down, even if that makes me late to work,
or a date, or a flight, or life in general. This is the price I pay to access the magic you are.
I willingly accept it because you soothe in me the things that medication,
professional achievements, sex, wine, and food never will...
You bring me peace through perspective and give the fire inside me a voice.
You hold space for my fears, demons, traumas, insecurities, longings, and voids
to have productive conversations with the rest of me.
Do you have any idea how many fights you have helped quell inside me?
How many dead ends have you helped me describe in vivid detail?
How many times my heart has used you to unload my burdens?
You gave my emotions the ability to speak the same language.
You are the friend that is never too tired to hear about my feelings.
You are the map I used to come home to myself when the GPS fails me.
If that is not magic, I don't know what is.

When Tiny Warriors Break Pinatas

They stand in a line from tallest to shortest
One by one, the tiny warriors take their turns
swinging sticks, conquering fears, breaking curses,
jumping for joy, receiving sweet abundance.
They sing their battle cry in affirming unison
Dale, Dale, Dale! iNo pierdas el tiro!
Porque si lo pierdes, pierdes el camino
Until one of the warriors breaks it for good.

Our ancestors used to make piñatas out of clay
They adorned them with feathers for the god of war
Missionaries added the tissue paper and the rules
Saying the points on these stars were for each deadly sin
propaganda designed to tame us with conversion
Did they not realize our elders never
Stopped training tiny warriors for battle?
They taught us to wield sticks with strength
and made it look like an innocent game.

When tiny warriors break piñatas
it teaches them that breaking some things
create sweet, sweet abundance for everyone
it teaches them that that some things must be broken
like barriers, cycles of oppression, and psychological cages
It teaches them that when you break these things hard enough
you can carry away with you all the abundance that is meant for you
along with the new ancestral wisdom gained in the battle to acquire it.

When the tiny warriors inside us break piñatas
the earth vibrates and our ancestors smile
They clap and sing our beloved battle cry to us
Dale, Dale, Dale! iNo pierdas el tiro!
Porque si lo pierdes, pierdes el camino
Our response is the sound of the seeds
they planted finally blooming gardens of liberation.

Breakdown

When my breakdown started, I felt invincible
I was overflowing with energy and ideas
I couldn't keep my hands off things I couldn't afford
My anxiety did such an amazing job acting like joy
She could have won an Oscar and a Golden Globe

The next phase of the breakdown was darkness
This is the part where your brain and body
simultaneously shut down the way a laptop does
in the middle of you typing the best sentence ever
and you push all the buttons but nothing happens
Your mind, your breath, your sense of reality
turn off all at once, and you have no control
There is no way to power yourself back up
you just have to wait there with blank stare, blinking,
crying, screaming and eventually breathing
while praying that something wakes you up again

The next phase of the breakdown was hunger
I needed to eat everything I saw on the menu
I needed to talk up a storm to make up for lost time
I needed to...but my brain was still buffering
I short-circuited and lost ability to speak
I could only express myself in writing
Somehow part of me knew this might happen
because I had index cards and a pen in my purse
but I have no idea how they got there

The next phase of the breakdown was index cards
I pulled them out and started writing
First, I just wrote how I was feeling
    I feel stuck
        I can't breath
            I want more Mac & Cheese

Until my written thoughts became equal parts ridiculous and intense

I think I have an idea that will win me a Nobel Peace Prize

> *I am going to write the most amazing poem and email it to Lin Manuel Miranda. He is going to love it and put it in his next musical*

I don't think I went to bed last night.

> *I am going to write poems for Cardi B's songs and DM them to her on Instagram until we're best friends*

I haven't taken my meds in 3 days.

> *I am going to get a MacArthur genius grant or die trying.*

I can feel myself going crazy.

> *I don't have a million-dollar idea, just a lot of thousand dollar ones.*

I don't know how to stop it.

The next phase of the breakdown was crying
So…..much……. crying……
over everything that ever happened to me ever
I picked apart every wound and every scab
weeping and grieving with my whole body
I held myself, my inner child, my inner teen
All of us broken, bruised, and barely breathing

The next phase of the breakdown was beige
This is the part of where ambulances show up
After you showed up to a networking brunch
crying in your pajamas talking about sad shit
And then didn't answer your phone for 2 days
Friends come to check on you, crying at the state you're in,
Hospitals are involved, emergency contacts get called,
and the meds you take result in a delicious nap

The next phase of the breakdown is recovery…
I am still figuring that phase out.

Dreams and Magic

How do I crack open the memories inside of me?
I grew up in a home with two parents
and a set of incomplete encyclopedias
all doing the best they could

The universe is only so big
when all you can reference is a bible
and the letters X, W, U, and P
Poverty took the rest of the alphabet from us
I had to find a way to to get it back.
Didn't I?

I didn't touch a wood scrabble tile
until I was well in to my 20s
As a baby birds and butterflies
never once circled me
How in the world did I learn to spell
the vocabulary of dreams and magic?

How was I supposed to know the best way to
make music let alone keep it inside of me?
I only remember being told about the way
my Apá used to sing to me as a baby.
Perhaps that should have been enough
to trigger a muscle memory.

Letting Go

I am letting go
of traditions that never served me
of family secrets
of curses swept under the rug
of the people I love but can't save
of other people's bullshit

I am letting go
of my inner imposter
of my past mistakes
of my need for control
of my desire to be perfect
of timelines and deadlines

I'd rather be leaping into a life
where passion, purpose, and paycheck
form a sacred alliance for my highest good
into my spiritual renaissance
into my rich Tia vibes
into the unknown

I'd rather be pushing forward
with faith and no map
with occasional patience
with consistent commitment
with wisdom I've collected
with spirit as my guide

I will be arriving
even if I get there late
even if I am as slow as a snail
even if I am as old as a turtle
The party will not start
until I get there anyway

As My Heart Becomes Free

As my heart becomes free
my body turns to clay
Metamorphosis begins
I mold myself into awakening

I turn myself from plate to pitcher
from flat surface to curvy vessel
Something that can fill and be filled

As my heart becomes free
I break molds and reinvent traditions
I start architecting dreams into existence
I become the prophecy my ancestors spoke of

My eyes blink open to greet the light
I walk Into the world palms facing up
ready to receive my backlog of blessings

Diana Medina

Love

I felt it in my chest
crying in the darkness
It smelled like safety

I felt it in the hands
cradling my teary face
It sounded like calm

I feel it in the absence
when I crave a warm touch
It always tastes bittersweet

Belief Practice

Say it
I am worthy
I am beautiful
I am capable
I am qualified
I am guided
I am... trying to be
Wanting to be
Hoping to be
Being it
Speak it enough times
until you act like it
Act like it until you can't
Then stop
Take a breath
Now start again
from the top

Roots, Raises

I put my hands on the ground to hold hands with Mother Earth.

> *"I've got you. I always have."*

"Even when I walked all over you mindlessly?"
I am surprised by her kind acceptance.

> *"Especially then."*

My eyes welled up with tears of regret as I asked for her forgiveness.

> *"No need. There is nothing to forgive. Love moved you to lose yourself. Isn't it also love that moved you to find yourself again? Isn't that why you came to see me?"*

I began to shake as every limb on my body nodded in agreement

We continued holding hands staring at one another's eyes
mine brown like dirt, hers green like grass.
I felt her warmth kissing the skin on my fingertips.

She filled my brain with calm
filled my heart with purpose
filled my eyes with clarity
She prepared my soil for a harvest
of growth and joy beyond my wildest dreams.

I felt the seeds of possibilities bury themselves
in my womb, my limbs, my mind, and my blood.
The wind whispered the coordinates of my destiny into my ears.
In the midst of this magic, I still felt lost and overwhelmed

> *"Your soul speaks my language and will always know the way"*

"How is that possible? I am so confused.
I don't know what you're saying right now.
How will I know the way later?"

> *"Listen to the trees and the moonlight. All of their wisdom will seep into your skin and cuddle your bones until you sigh in relief.*
> *If the clutter and noise of the world don't let you see the way, I will make your toes wiggle so you can feel the earth begin to shift beneath your feet.*
> *I will send your nose the smell of wet soil to awaken you.*
> *I will fill your ears with songs of your ancestors to affirm your strength.*
> *I will inspire you to move by sending you all the divine coding you need.*
> *But you must promise something."*

"What?" I ask.
I knew there was a catch.
There is always a catch.

> *"The journey will not be easy. You must promise that you will be fully prepared to walk through an uphill mountain of shit to get to your paradise. This is the only way to come home to yourself."*

Under the full moon, I promise her I will stay the course.
And with remnants of Mother Earth under my fingernails,
I move forward in search of my new home in paradise.

Heal Me Faster

I am in a hurry to heal and afraid at the same time
Being paralyzed by fear and worried about what
is waiting on the other side of healing really sucks.

Contrary to what spiritual Instagram posts
would have you believe, awakenings are sloppier
and dustier than cleaning out a cluttered garage.

I know there's a goddess in me somewhere,
but what am I supposed to do when
some days she doesn't want to shower
or eat or put on pants or go to work?

There is no filter that speeds up this process
There is only waiting

When you are in a hurry to heal, you are stuck
wading between fear and worry, everything sucks.
Life is stuck in a boomerang loop
going from one to the other over and over

Instead of patiently waiting for the healing,
you tighten your grips around your hurt
You retreat into a suffocating sphere of inner influence
because having control there is better than waiting.

You are way too hurt and too anxious to be patient.
too tired to be resilient and too annoyed to wait for your blessings
You want them all, and you want them fast.

God looks at your tantrum smiling and says, "that's nice."

10 de Mayo

On every Mother's Day
Nobody, not even god,
gives an almost-mother anything
Not a gift
Not a hug
Not an explanation
Not even a good reason

So, if we see each other today
don't be surprised
If all I can give you is an excuse
for why I can't make it to brunch
It's not because of you
It's because today
it's just too hard to go outside

One every Mother's Day
I remember
the day I missed my carriage
Because of that day
I spend this day crying
over what could have been

On every Mother's Day
I wonder what it would feel like to be called mommy.
How old would my carriage be had I not missed it?
How exhausted would I be from taking care of it?
How big would I be smiling right now receiving
a piece of my carriage's heart covered in macaroni and glitter?

On every Mother's Day
I think this day could've been special
instead of what it is;
A day when I really, really, really miss my carriage
A day when members of a club I will never be a part of
consume greeting cards, flowers, and eggs Benedict

A day about celebrating something
I am no longer built to do
A day I spend trying not to vomit at the taste
of bittersweet politeness on my lips

I avoid everything on this day
Instagram
Eye contact
Television
Stores
People
All of it

On every Mother's Day
I hold my hands in frozen fists
until my nails leave deep
imprints on my palms

I shut my eyes good and tight
I cover my ears all day and night
I purse my lips for dear, dear life
I vow to keep my tears to myself

On every Mother's Day
doing all of that
is the easiest hard thing I can do.

These Lips

These lips...
are full
fuller than my email inbox
fuller than a trash can
fuller than a Costco shopping cart
they take up   half the real-estate on my face

These lips...
go through lots of chapstick,
conversations, and
catcalls from vulgar men
who take one look at them
and loudly holler, "Damn girl!!
Look at those pretty lips.
I bet you suck good dick."
These interactions are the
conversational equivalent to
receiving an unsolicited dick pic
in the middle of my trips to unsexy places
like the dentist, the dog park, or CVS.

These lips...
are a sacred space on my face.
When I hear those comments
I feel quiet flows of anger moving
from my feet to my fingertips
like the red liquid in a thermometer
rising on a scorching hot day
I am appalled at the audacity of such men

In response I want to say,
How dare you?
Who raised you?
You kiss your wife, sisters, daughters, and
mommas with that mouth, don't you?
I bet your mind is a perverted cesspool

of unbecoming thoughts, and they have no idea.

I want to say,
You know what these lips do?
They inspire people,
They say prayers,
They smile when I am happy,
They tremble when I am hurt,
They create verbal constellations
of words and expressions that
your manhood could never comprehend.

I want to say,
You know what else these lips do?
They speak truth to power,
They sing songs,
They kiss nieces and nephews,
They hum meaning and melody into the world

They are...
a gift from my mother
a trademark of my ancestry
and my weapon of choice in every battle
I have to fight as a woman in this world.

I spit more fire out of these lips
than Khaleesi's three dragons combined.
So, you best believe that if your dick ever
had the   divine pleasure of entering
this temple on my face,
you'd nut the moment you make contact.

These lips
are a plush pink megaphone
from which I spit verbal Viagra
Your dick wouldn't be able to handle it.
They are not here to give your dick
something you did not earn

These lips...
are attached to me
a whole person, with a heart and
a mind that is its own magical universe
They are more than just an orifice
to be used for pleasure and then discarded
by something as insignificant, uneventful,
and underwhelming as your dick.

These lips...
are a universe of truth.
They inquire and inspire
motivate and advocate
say grace and tell jokes

In any given moment they can
shine bright, show love, shift perspectives,
fuel passions, fight fires, or free minds.

These lips...
can burn you
or they can bless you
it all depends on your approach.

You'd be wise to proceed with respect
or get the fuck out of my face.

Diana Medina

Rubbing Lotion on my Skin

When I do it, I imagine I am marinating myself in softness
When this creamy substance seeps into my pores
I hope it makes me taste more tender and smell more sweet
I want it to make me fall off my own bones
so my lovers can make a meal out of me
I hope eventually it makes someone think
I feel like a place they can call home

I do it so much my shadow and reflection
have become jealous they can't touch me
If the only hands that ever touch me this way are my own
I hope they will always be friendly

I'm tired of enduring harm by my own hands
tired of parts of my skin feeling foreign
no longer wanting to be a stranger to myself
I want these hands, my hands, to hold me
to love every curve and crevice on this body
until my spirit becomes one with my skin

Doing it now is like rubbing prayers into my flesh
May my knees and elbows never know ash
May my face and hands never know dryness
May my neck never know wrinkles
May my palms and fingers be affirmations
saying, "I love you" when I rub myself
with these creamy scented ointments
May they make me as soft as I am strong
as moisturized as I am realized
as fragrant as I am free

Ritual Bath

Rose petals scattering
Red, white, pink, yellow
Soaking and colorful
Floating in circles
Bathtub full of water
Music full of poetry
Me, naked and vulnerable
watching them swim around me
Some stick to me
others touch me softly
They feel like gentle kisses
all over on my brown skin
I cry backlogs of tears
illuminated by candlelight
I wonder, is this what self-love is?

Alma's Passport

A past life is like your soul's passport
Your body is the travel vessel
This life, your life, is the vacation you are going on together
This moment is your awakening

Let's call your soul.... Alma

This passport shows you where Alma has been
It gives you context for where you can go
to heal your things and also visit her things...
sometimes her things will look like your things
when that happens, that's a repeating pattern
Like eating at different restaurants and always ordering the same mistake

This passport is like a divine guidebook to plan your eternal vacation...
your life.
Alma's passport is like a treasure map, Yelp, Craigslist, Amazon, Groupon, karmic online banking, a dating app, and a flashlight all rolled into one.

Trauma is like sharing a suitcase with Alma.
Sometimes Alma leaves used undies in there.
You don't have to wear them, but you should make sure to wash them with yours because
eventually you will end up wearing them by accident.

Watermelon Dodgeball

I purchased a watermelon
entirely too big for me to eat alone
It rolled out of the shopping bag
like a green fruity wrecking ball
It didn't even fit in my tiny little fridge

The downside of ordering groceries
is delegating the picking of my fruits
into the hands of some stranger
Many would say this is a good reason
to not order groceries online
but in the midst of a pandemic
and in the depths of my despair
I can't bring myself to go to the store

I just wanted a small watermelon
One I could enjoy as a party of one
What I got was one the size of a dodgeball
just like the one that gave me nightmares
in elementary school… I was never athletic.
I always got picked second to last that game
The bright side? There was one girl in my class
who was worse at dodgeball than I was
I should have been friends with her, but I wasn't

Church Songs

I still remember some church songs
I don't remember the sermons
The lessons or the warnings from el Padre
I don't remember the prayers or lecturas
I don't remember the rules... what is sin, what is not.

But the songs they sang between routines
of standing, kneeling, contemplating are
the few things that will forever take up space
in the hidden dusty file cabinets of my brain

Yo no soy nada y del polvo nací
Pero tu me amas y moriste por mi
I am nothing, and I was born of dirt
But you love me, and you died for me

That is all I needed to hear to know
that I can live however I need to
that god will speak to me in my language
that bible pages are not the only place where word of god is
and priests aren't the only ones with the power
to speak life into the heart of the needy and hurting

If I am nothing, If I was was born from dirt
then, I am part Mother Earth, and she is part of me
By that logic, why can't hiking and gardening be my church?
Why must I go to ornate buildings to kneel and repeat things
like a robot to prove my faith is real?
To prove that god speaks to me too?

Señor me has mirado a los ojos
Sonriendo has dicho mi nombre
Lord, you've looked into my eyes
You've smiled and said my name

Why can't that be enough?
Why then must there also be rules and regulations
to the way I honor what is divine in me?
If god has looked into my eyes, smiled, and said my name
does it not stand to reason that we can communicate without
all that inflexible bureaucracy tradition demands we hold on to?
Without judgements? Without the uncomfortable claims that
there is only one right way? Without the constant question of those of us
who are on infinite searches for universal truth?
Their rules make no difference if the only universal truth is love
and our search for it? That starts within ourselves....
That is not sinful or selfish; That is just me coming home to myself learning
to worship what is divine in me, in the temple that I am.

Does the church not wonder how many sheep they have wounded by
telling the world there is only one right way?
Does the church not wonder how our ancestors have been dismissed
when they were too busy forsaking those other faiths, deities, explanations
of the divine that came before Christ?

Ama always tells me she wants to see me walking
en los caminos de dios... in god's paths
She says, "Tu puedes ser predicadora" (you can be a preacher)
I say, "No, yo prefiero ser poeta... (I'd rather be a poet)

If these words I write can speak to hearts,
if these words I write can heal me,
if these words I write can heal others,
then every book I write them in,
and every mic I speak them into is my church,
my congregation, my connection to the lost sheep.

Poetry is my rallying cry for the prodigal children,
the ones they call lost, selfish, sinners, black sheep.
I am all of them. They are my congregation:

My poetry is for them. That is how the divine flows in me.

If this is my gift, then who am I to stop it?
Who are they to tell me it's not good enough, not godly enough?
Is poetry not part of our creation story?
Am I not made of dirt and of the earth?
Did God not look into my eyes and say my name?
These words, these feelings, these aches....
These fragments of my soul in poetic form belong to God,
they belong to me, because we are one in the same.

Sarape Lovers

Under cover of sarape
two lovers hide from the world
taking vacations in one another's eyes
shoulder to shoulder, thigh to thigh
Where one body ends and the other begins
is a welcome unknown

Under cover of sarape
there is no work or pain
The only expectation is breathing
There are only the napes of neck
graze of thigh, warmth of body
giggles and secrets
inside jokes, messed up hair

Under the cover of sarape
stripes replace starry skies
Cotton becomes shelter
People become homes
Getting lost in the universe
They created together, time stops
There is only warmth here

Under the cover of sarape
feet always stay firmly planted
on the floor, on the earth,
on reality....as beautiful as it here
This shelter in only temporary

Long Receipts

If the world is a giant supermarket
then the creator is the cashier
Ancestors and deities stock the shelves
Our souls are the shoppers
Our bodies, the shopping carts
We browse this place looking for passions, for answers, for clarity
Sometimes we find darkness, despair, and distractions
We unload our purchases onto
the divine, inter-dimensional conveyor belt
It moves us towards a galaxy of infinite check-out stands
Our souls' purchases fall through cracks sometimes
some because they are traumas
some because they are burdens
some because they are balls
All must be released
so nothing keeps weighing us down
What remains in our essence
our awakenings, our faith, our wisdom
Creator watches us scan those items on the registers
The total we owe has already been paid
The length of our receipts within us

Creator and Crayons

When the creator was a child
all the gardens were painted with crayons
Whimsy and joy were the requirement
to tiptoe within them
Technicolor dinosaurs, bugs, bees and frogs
sang De Colores at the top of their lungs
As the Flowers grew taller than the mountains
because that is what flowers do, they grow

When the creator was a child
all the plants and bugs were summoned here
They danced together and talked about coloring
They agreed that inspiration has no rules
and beauty has no boundaries
They planted crops of crayons together
and took turns coloring the sides of mountains
and tops of skies with their colorful harvest

Changes

Eyes close
Inhale the moment
Exhale anxiety
Wipe tears

Nothing is wrong
Yet everything is

I've watched myself
Becoming
Different
Before my eyes

I feel mild dread
I wonder: What if?
I don't know me anymore

Mundane Magic

Dump trucks come down the alley
distinct weekday morning melody
metal, motor, machine, my alarm clock
disrupting dreams still in progress

Toes wiggle saying it's time
My body doesn't want it to be
Hit snooze, just five more minutes
repeat cycle three more times
until rising is inevitable, feet finally touch floor

Water splashes on face, an H2O wakeup call
Contemplate poetic power of toothpaste
minty, exhilarating, flavor enhanced spit
brush, smile with creamy coating
remove tartar, refresh breath, reveal shine
wash out words from last night's dream

With mouth prepared to spit new wisdom
we prepare to throw our face into the world
All of this routine is mundane, yet magical
proof that a new start is always a day away

Kisses from the Sun

Today my weary body rises
finally ready to meet courage
I take a step with her outside.

I am still in pajamas and slippers,
my head adorned with a crown
of crazy hair in full greñuda glory.

Wrapped a blanket, sunglasses on
I take my deepest breath of the week
as sun rays lovingly kiss my face.

I exhale raising my chin to the sky
my skin rejoices, "Thank you, Mija.
I was thirsty for a dosage of new light."

Your Calling

Your calling doesn't give a fuck
about your nerves or insecurities.

Your calling doesn't understand
anxiety or timing or tact or bills.

Your calling has 1000 cell phones and
redial is her favorite button to push.

Your calling will just call   and call   until
you are brave or desperate enough to answer.

So answer already... your calling has all day.

Diana Medina

Immortal Amá

*"No me puedo morir sin tener
uno de tus hijos en mis brazos"*
I cannot die without holding
one of your children in my arms
I cannot count the number of times
I have heard my mother say
She said it to my big brother a lot
living as a bachelor in their house
in a room with his own entrance
No one stood guard of his virginity
or virtue. No one does that to men.
He married after strings of girlfriends
and that comment was passed on to me

*"No me puedo morir sin tener
uno de tus hijos en mis brazos"*
She started to say it right after I got married
like a reminder to remember the objective
when it took me 3 years to get pregnant
when I had a miscarriage
when my marriage ended in divorce
when my body said motherhood was not for me
and my heart eventually came around to agree
She'd say, *"No, no, no, Mija!
Dios tiene la última palabra"*
God has the final say...
All these roadblocks sound like a final says to me.

*"Yo no me puedo morir sin tener
uno de tus hijos en mis brazos"*
I cannot die without holding
one of your children in my arms
Every time I hear her say it
I feel like a daughter shaped disappointment
The best I can do to deal with this phrase
that stings my ears is to remember that

as long as I am infertile she will be immortal
Of all the benefits of not having children
an immortal mother is definitely one of them.
I could go about my life...
just me, my Chihuahua,
a career, a disposable income
maybe even a lover sometimes
galavanting with purpose all over the world
being able to live liberated for the both of us
guarded by my immortal mothers prayers

Prayers like "que todo te salga bien"
May everything go well for you
That's it... simple, powerful, all encompassing
Bien is good, and todo is a lot of stuff
Todo is everything. Todo is work,
a love life, therapy, healing, raised vibration,
self confidence, self love, good sex, big orgasms,
full confidence in all the choices I make from my gut
"Que todo, todo, todo te salga bien, mija"

Todo is everything...
the only thing strong enough to protect everything
are the prayers of an immortal mother.

Ode to my Lonjas

Oh beloved pelota of flesh
You remind me I am expanding
Jeans not closing is a small price to pay
for the warmth of tamales and pans dulce inside me
I call the contemplations that come to me
when you are full: panzamientos

Because of you I am sturdy and grounded
I have cushion when I fall
I will never be carried away by the wind
At night when it's cold, I hold you in my hands
and remember I've always had you

A woman once asked me when my baby was due.
I held you as I looked at her and said,
"I am not with child, I am with burrito.
It was good. I am due to shit it out
sometime tomorrow around 10am…"
She was embarrassed. I was proud.

On dates you encourage me to eat like I mean it.
"Eat those wings con ganas and sabor!" you say.
"Lambete los dedos en frente de este hombre!
I want to taste the bbq sauce and he wants to see
your tongue and fingers enjoying themselves!"

You say, "Go ahead and post a full body pic on that dating app
Let them see how much space we take up"
You remind me that gordita me veo más bonita
así rellenita bien comidita
You encourage me to let it be known
that I take big bites out of life and sandwiches
You remind me to let beauty be shown
when I fill out a pair of leggings because
my magical body is worthy of beholding

When I'm naked in front of lovers you look them in the eye with confidence
Saying go ahead grab me, you know you want to,
every man wants to feel a handful of carne shaped abundance.

Lonjita, you are the perfect wingwoman for my titties and my soul.

Rose

It comes in many colors
Red for passion
Black for mystery
White for what is still pure

A rosey thorn, a thorny rose
It is neither, it is both
I get pricked every time
I hold this beauty too long

One moment a release
the next an inconvenience
But something familiar
is better than nothing

Recognition makes it easy
to forget the magic
of newly emerging things

Family Curses

the bitterness gene
gets passed around
for one it lasts a moment
for one it lasts a lifetime

this anger is contagious
it festers in hearts
fulfilling prophecies
planted in imaginations

undoing its victims
slowly and steadily
it turns prayers obsolete
it makes faith a decoration

so potent, so deep
a dead victim will rise
to kick people out
of their funeral service

saying don't grieve me
don't miss me, don't look at me
just leave me here rotting
with my righteous anger

Diana Medina

An Orgasmic Prayer

The first one I had was for all the times
I never had one,
the times I just lied there dry as a desert,
letting my world go unrocked thinking,
Is this what all the fuss is about?
for the moments I felt ugly and undesirable
for the times I was utterly underwhelmed by boys
masquerading as men, safe places, or good lovers
for the parts of my body that had no idea
they were capable of floods and earthquakes
for all the affirmations I needed to see and feel
in order finally accept I was worthy of pleasure

All the orgasms I've had since are retroactive payback
for the ones my mother and grandmothers never had
for all the times they just lay there believing sex was sinful
and enjoying themselves made them putas
for the ways they were led to believe their bodies were nothing but vessels for procreation and male pleasure instead of what they truly were: centers of creation, homes for humanity, beacons of strength, catalysts of courage, divinity in human form. They were goddesses completely unaware of how much men feared them.

Just like we must remember where we come from we must also remember who we cum for: this is what it means to heal ourselves, our wombs, and our lineages.
Every orgasm we have is liberation for us and for them ladies:
our mothers, grandmothers, tias, hermanas, all of them.
Let us collect them one after another, after another, after another.
Let us store them in stockpiles of pleasure to make as
offerings to every goddess in our lineage in the altars between our legs. May we never allow ourselves to
feel unworthy or go unpleased ever again.

And may we all say... Amen.

Lust Partner

Maybe you weren't my soulmate
But as a lust partner you were superb
I woke up craving smooth skin
and there you were, the color of caramel
ready to smother every inch of me
You were shining, your lust orbiting mine
I was the moon, you were the sun
Our bodies made an eclipse
Your hands were on my hips
I was biting your lower lip,
all the faucets in my basement dripped
You were Noa, I was the arc
You stayed inside me during the flood
I swam in you and we drowned together
You used my honey to sweeten your tea
Rested your face on my mountains
We broke curses, fought demons,
Made our mumbles prayers of ecstasy
Worshiped each other's holy temples
I learned how to live frozen in time,
surrendering to only the present
taking my pleasure and having seconds
because I am my own soul mate
I am worthy, blessed, highly favored, and
will call you when I need your services again

Mundane Magic

dump trucks come down the alley
distinct weekday morning melody
metal, motor, machine, my alarm clock
all disrupting dreams still in progress

toes wiggle saying it's time
my body doesn't want it to be
hit snooze, just five more minutes
repeat cycle three more times
until rising is inevitable, feet finally touch floor

water splashes on face, an H2O wakeup call
contemplate poetic power of toothpaste
minty, exhilarating, flavor enhanced spit
brush smile with creamy coating
remove tartar, refresh breath, reveal shine
wash out words from last night's dream

with mouth prepared to spit new wisdom
prepared to throw clean face into the world
all of this routine is mundane yet magical
proof that a new start is always a day away

Apartments

This apartment talks to me
I listen for what it asks of me
Call me crazy but
All of my apartments talk to me

They ask things of me
They say I can't occupy them
Unless I am willing to have
A conscious relationship
with them and myself
within 4 walls

I sit in every corner
I imagine myself breathing here
Looking around considering
What is in my line of sight
What is in my line of vibration

It tells how to live in her
How to honor her
How to honor myself
And so I do

Babysitting

I am my inner child's full-time babysitter
Some days she is a pouty mocosa mimada
wanting what she wants having no patience
She throws loud tantrums in the corners of the rooms
I try to live my life in when she has to wait for things

Other days she is a delightful pain in the ass
A loud, impulsive, messy, smiling goofball
asking to be seen, acknowledged, held, accepted
We learn to trust each other by solving puzzles together
We have ice cream for breakfast and never comb our hair

These days it's hard to tell who is who
Hard to see where she ends and I begin
Hard to know who is actually in charge
Maybe that's the point

Abuelitas & Trenzas

I wear a trenza
solo una
long and black it hangs, kissing
my neck, spine, and back

My abuelitas wore trenzas,
Dos, siempre dos
thick and long and silver
Adorning their shoulders
framing their faces

When I wear my trenza
I pull my hair out of my face
because it's time to get to work
I tell myself to live, vive
Sin vergüenza

Abuelitas:
No se preocupen
No estoy perdida
I hold each of you when
I braid your smiles into my hair
Your love covers my backbone

Miren como vuelo
I do all this wandering for you
I do all this dreaming for you
Do you see me flying?
Do you see how all of your shame
has died with me?

Abuelitas:
I am your do-over,
That thing you daydreamed about
Esta vida mía es su segunda oportunidad
What should I do with all this freedom?
¿Cual trauma vamos a sanar primero?

Sweet Revenge

I have no plans on pining for him
I have no plans of hating on your life
Why should I?
You think you found yourself a prince
But what you married was a parasite.

You can have him
He is my gift to you
Take him far away
Get him off the streets
Keep him away from good women
He's cursed
We don't want him

The most beautiful revenge
I can think of is that you stay with him
Take that bullet for us all
As the years   pass, you will see what I saw
How slowly the facade of his love cracks
Even the best actors can't play a role forever

I am not crying for him
I am not suffering
I am thriving
I am free

I've never been a fan of being compared
Setting bars is more my style, always has been
You'll learn what I learned soon enough

Go ahead
Fix him
Love him
Do whatever you like
You'll be doing it in my shadow
He will compare you to me
for better or worse.

Womb, Temple, or Tomb?

My body is a temple
I pray to saints that live
among the ruins of my womb
They tell me The Creator wanted things this way
They said my destiny is to break toxic cycles
to make sure these family traumas die with me

They say:
you are the one we have chosen
our village's traumas and toxic traditions
all of them die with you
you are the cycle breaker
the reinventor
the paver of a new path
the maker of word filled legacies
you are destined to love souls
to breathe   life into those who lost it
those who sleep while going through the motions of life

In every family there is a chosen one
whose womb is destined for greater things
A misunderstood breaker of cycles
A reinventor, a paver of new paths
Ancestral traumas and toxic traditions
All of them will die in their hands
They will turn these things into clay
They will use them to create something new
To breathe   life into those who lost it
To awaken those who sleep among the living
That is why people call them too much
and beg them to stay small and fit into boxes
Abundance like theirs can never be contained
It must simply run its course for all of our sakes

Mi cuerpo es un templo
Rezo a los santos que viven entre las ruinas de mi vientre
Me dicen que asi queria Dios las cosas
Dicen que mi destino es romper ciclos tóxicos para así asegurar que estos traumas familiares mueren conmigo.

I named you Milagro

I named you Milagro because
if my miscarriage had a theme song
It would be the song Vida by La Mafia
The melody makes me think of you
Every time I hear it on the car radio
The words hit me so hard
I have to pull over to weep

I named you Milagro because
the Vatican declares recoveries miraculous
when they are complete and instantaneous
when they heal and free someone of demons
when they raise someone from the dead
If El Papa would have seen what went down
during the ultrasound when I met and lost you
he would agree there is no other explanation.

I named you Milagro because
Now I know what Mary felt when God
gave their only son as payment for strangers' sins.
God took you from me the same way he took
Jesus from Mary for a higher purpose
Just like them, you and I, shared a body but
you were also not meant for this world.
You were meant to only inhabit me, my body
Your short presence and permanent absence
turned my weary womb into a temple.

I named you Milagro because a Medium
once told me you made it to the other side
That you were safe with my ancestors
looking down on me as I attempt to carry on.
Some days I look at the calendar and think of you
How old would you have been?

Diana Medina

What milestone might I be witnessing?
In what way would you be challenging me today?
A part of me will always ache for you, MIlagro

I named you Milagro because
I love you more than the air I breathe
My heart opened when I saw you
A lentil sized speckle on a screen
I didn't start living until I lost you
I never thought a life so short
could have such profound meaning

I named you Milagro because
I'd be lying if I said I don't think about it sometimes
What it would be like to be the protector of a little soul
Something that loves me because it's   part of me
A piece of my heart walking through the world
But that life, motherhood, is not for me anymore

I named you Milagro because
I did not arrive at the decision lightly
I arrived at the decision kicking and screaming
Resisting the calling from Spirit
Questioning the directive from God

I named you Milagro because you saved me
You set me free from a life not meant for me
removed me from people who were not equipped
to love me, support me, walk this life with me
You gave me the grand purpose of loving souls
My whole life will be a dance of gratitude for you

Anxiety

People think you can just make it stop,
control it, or politely ask it to leave.
They say it will go away if you just
Work out
Drink water
Don't think about it?

I wish ignoring this unwanted roommate
was simply about movement and hydration
Anxiety moved in with me years ago
without asking my permission
Her name is on the lease of my whole being
She leaves her dirty dishes in the sink
She never cleans up after herself

I try to go out to get away from her, but
she sticks to me like gum on my shoe
She comes with me everywhere I go
Leaving trails is sticky tentative residue
She questions everything I do and say
before and after I do and say it
She worries about everything… always
Claiming it's to keep me safe
But all it does is keep me guessing.

She adds her filter to every photo I take,
every landmark I visit, every milestone I have.
Because of her, I never know what is real
what is imagined, what is growth,
what is work, and what is a blessing
She is the reason I feel like too much
and not enough at the same time.

New Chapters

New chapters are hard to start
Turning a page sounds simple
Until you feel the massive weight
of a page between your fingertips
In that moment a sliver of a tree
covered in ink can weigh 1,000 tons

Many things contribute to that weight
Clutter of possessions from lives past
Unanswered question and texts
Boxes of clothing that no longer fit
Heartbreak over words unexpressed

My tears can fill 5 gallon jugs over and over
I grieve for people who don't feel safe anymore,
for who I used to be, for things that didn't work out
I watch the chasm between my future and the past
grow bigger and bigger until going back to that girl
feels scarier than moving forward towards fresh starts
My comfort zone shrinks as I leave it in the distance
The vast unknown of a fresh start stares me in the face

Before it can be an adventure to take joy in
Starting over is an experiential process of
unburdening, grieving, remembering, forgetting
Joy can't come until the darkness leaves

Marijuana

A medicine
A confidant
A writer's jet fuel
A sacred herb

I remember you come from earth
I think you must know my ancestors
I touch you with my fingers
To feel closer to them and myself
As I say my three favorite prayers:
Help
Thanks
Wow

The ceremony continues
Light incense, cleanse
Light palo santo, cleanse
Light joint, cleanse
Inhale, magic
exhale, magic
ponder, magic
write, poetry

Ode to Santa Marijuana

She visits me in my dazes
When I put myself in them
This has slowly become
the only self care ritual
that makes sense to me.

Santa Marijuana
Verde como los bosques
Sacerdota de humo y fuego
Llena mi olfato de claridad
Dame la locura que me falta
para hacer de esta vida mía
un desmadre digno y divino

I reach for her box
Pull out our favorite tools
music, grinder, stick, spoon
I let her caress my finger tips
as I pack her into paper cones
I mumble prayers under my breath
between puffs of her medicine
I wait for the smoke to clear
my body to sink   and
I am slapped in the face
by a whirlwind of relaxation
when her scent   enters the room

Santa Marijuana
Oscura como la tierra
Limpia mis recuerdos con tu magia
Llena mi cerebro de ideas frescas
Ayúdame a encontrar los poemas de la vida
entre mis respiraciones más profundas

I crave her guidance
when to do lists overpower me

when my energy feels stagnant
when I need something to unstick me
so certainty and ideas can flow again
and the woman I see in the mirror
can let go and dance again

Santa Marijuana appears
Eyes red, hair messy
Skin clear, bright smile
Twinkles in her bloodshot eyes
With hands full of snacks
Cheetos, donuts, tacos, cake
Salty, sweet, savory, rich

I stare at her, at the snacks, at the mirror
She gives me advice between nibbles
When I get too paranoid to trust myself
She looks me in my red eyes
We mirror one another's movements
Dancing together in slow motion

I ask her all my questions
Quickly, one after another
Afraid we will run out of time
What does it mean when people call me too much?
Shouldn't I be offended?
Do you think my dog has thoughts?
Wouldn't it be cool to do poems in autotune?
Is this why I am still single?

She puts her hands up
Blowing her smoke in my face
She issues her proclamation
As she hands me a snack.
"Ya, ya, ya... serena morena.
Ay muere la canción. Ya."

But I still have questions.
I need her to help me think.

I ask her about what I should do
about my future, about my past,
I don't know how to forgive myself
for not knowing what I didn't know.
I confess that I'm still paralyzed
with indecision, worry, and fear.

She blows more smoke in my face
Hands me more snacks and answers,
"Girl, why are you tripping?
You know I got you. You're good.
None of that matters. There is only now.
The past is a now that already happened.
The future is a now that hasn't happened yet.
Just surrender to this moment, cabrona."

I do as she says, like an obedient student
I Inhale, puff, exhale, the moment passes.
I push the pause button on my spiraling.
Lean into my curiosity as I go through the
Cluttered closets of my brain one by one.

Santa Marijuana
Paciente como hojas cambiando de color
Guíame hacia un despertar celestial
Plántame en un jardín con una nueva vida
Haz que flores y plantas broten de mi boca
y usaré sus colores vibrantes para decorar mi vida
Crearé un nuevo universo a mi alrededor

"Asi mero," she affirms "look within you.
Just like that. One closet at a time.
Una idea a la vez. Una locura a la vez.
Ideas are coming, money is coming,
good dick is coming, good fortune is coming.
The universe is coming all over you, Mija.
Lean back, smile, create, enjoy yourself.
And, please, for the love of Goddess
stop ruining your own high."

The Virtue of Vergüenza

The virtue of *vergüenza* (shame)
A Latino parent's favorite social construct
The finger that always pointed to tradition
The internal voice that told me what was expected
Vergüenza was the reason my parents reprimanded me
when I stirred the pot, when I asked for things,
when I took too many liberties in being myself
For better or worse this set of beliefs kept me in line
but being silent never sat right in my body
Waiting for permission to exist wasn't my style

I was taught *vergüenza* was something we all needed
to know what our place was on society's totem pole
Under this paradigm, me taking up any space at all
constituted misbehavior; reprimands included lines
repeated so often they felt like mantras for the silent:
Eso no se hace (that is not done)
No tengas tanta confianza (don't be so confident)
Somos gente humilde (we are humble people)
Somos honrados (we are honest people)
Hay que tener vergüenza (you have to have shame)

I didn't understand what shame had to do with anything
Why couldn't I be proud of who I was?
Why couldn't I ask for water when I was thirsty?
Why couldn't I be curious?
Why did I have to be quiet?
Why was my virtue connected to how much shame
my tiny shoulders could carry?
Hadn't my ancestors carried enough for us all?
Wasn't the point of living in America being free to speak?

The brown girl in the white room

Brown girl was nervous
It was her first time in a room this white
She wondered how they let her in
She worried she wouldn't know what the room knows
She wondered why she was here
Brown girl felt like a fly swimming in a jug of cream
trying to stay alive, afloat, adaptable

Brown girl has a special light switch
She can turn on light bulbs in people's minds
with just a question - asked thoughtfully at just the right time
Brown girl didn't know this was a gift until someone thanked her for it
She has spent her entire life trying to find her place in white rooms
Trying to silence her inner struggles so she can hear herself,
hear what the room is saying, and be part of the conversations
Her asking questions was just a way to buy herself some time
to silence her doubts before needing to say something more substantial

If the people in this white room could hear her
she would tell them the truth, finally confess,
Ladies and gentlemen my brain is a crowded conference room
My emotions and past selves show up daily to have heated debates
They question every thought I have before I ever say it
They argue about what is wrong today, so I can't put my finger on it
They question if I belong here with all of you
They call me an imposter
Their discourse is so loud it overpowers everything
From the sound of my breath moving through my nostrils
To the sound of my paycheck in my bank account,
To the sound of all of you talking about important things

A brain like this feels like the zoom call from hell
I am just a struggling facilitator
I feel like an inadequate holder of space
I try desperately to regain control of the dialogue
to steer these emotions towards harmony
But I fail every time I try, so on the outside I struggle to pay attention

I think maybe there is something I can do to be like all of you
or maybe this is what I have to deal with on my own
because I am just a brown girl in a very white room

My Secret Lies

My secret lies in the lies I tell myself
Lies like: I am not good enough,
I'm just ordinary,   nothing special.
In fact, no one wants or needs my opinion.
Who am I to speak and take up space?
What could I possibly say that someone
taller, thinner, kinder, lighter,
or more famous hasn't already said?

My secrets have lied to me.
They have kept me away
from my most authentic Self.
They have made me blind
to my own truth and afraid
of becoming powerful.
They made me hide my spark
under eurocentric expectations.
I sacrificed my substance
in hopes of being accepted.

My secret is I am trying.
In fact, me saying 1,000 ums
is the sound of me trying.
No one tries harder than me
when I speak all my truths.
Those ums are drums playing
the cadence of my convictions
as I learn to set them all free.
The moment I learned this truth
was the moment I came home
to myself; I settled into this skin
and it finally felt like safety.

My secret is that most of the time
I don't know what I am doing.
I haven't known what I am doing
for decades; I am so good at it.
People even listen to me sometimes.
They offer me seats at their tables.
They make space for my opinions.
They accuse me of inspiring them
to share bits and pieces of theirs.

My secret is I no longer believe
in faking it til I make it.
My only focus is making it,
being it, saying it, naming it
so that I never ever have
to fake anything again.

Panic Attack

Me in a red robe bleeding
Listening to sounds in an ER
I am not wearing pants
Where are my pants?
People keep saying, "Yes Ma'am"
Are they talking to me?
I remember the ambulance,
but how did I get here?

I see letters and symbols rearranging
my eyes are trying to tell me something
but my brain is not understanding
They say let go... we're here for you
Let go of what? Who is here?
I am confused, but I am also tired.
Maybe if I pass out something will save me.

I wake up rocking back and forth
breathing heavy, crying hard
my inhales and exhales so intense
they might control the weather
just like Storm from X-Men
but I'm no Hallie Berry
the storm is just inside me
I don't know how to stop it

I am in a disoriented dream state
As a woman in the next bed sings
Desde el cielo una hermosa mañana
La Guadalupana, La Guadalupana
The Latino people stop, smile,
and start looking at me... me??
I look around. Virgencita are you here?
Can you help me help myself?
What am I supposed to do now?

Hurting

Some days
My brain has too many tabs open
The thoughts don't stop
All of them want something from me
They overwhelm me

Some days
I ache for joy that isn't forced
I see the state of the world, chaos
I sink into the darkness
I hide and wallow
I wound myself out of spite
out of a little self-hatred,
out of unresolved anger
Such a frustrating way to ask god
to give me control of something

I seek temporary refuge in distractions
Forgetting about my burdens for a moment
Thinking maybe this time it will stick
Maybe this time my mind will quiet
Maybe today I will be able to breathe again
Laugh again, see again, be me again

Uterus

My uterus is not a crib
No little beings grow here
Their hearts don't beat
Their hands don't reach,
It's just stillness, not emptiness

My uterus is a file cabinet
filled to the brim with words
that will change the world and
traumas I haven't healed yet
They are all filed alphabetically by theme
in those hanging folders with colorful tabs
a tower of things to file sleeping in the inbox

Lost
Broken
Immature
Incomplete

                              Filed under: Things I am Not

Overflowing with ideas
Living things into existence

                              Filed under: Built this way

"You'll change your mind
when you meet the right man"

and

"You'll feel differently when your
 biological clock starts ticking"

                              Filed Under: No, I won't.

Preguntas para mi Abuelita

Abuelita Kika, solo te recuerdo
in snippets of foggy memories
en los ojos of that cute little brown
Chihuahua you sent to save me
They say its good luck to name pets
after people you love... so I did.

I remember seeing you in a tree
The day you passed away
Everyone forgot me but you didn't
Some thought I imagined you
But I saw you there, holding on to branches
head covered, waving goodbye to me
I wondered if it was you... It felt like you
but I never wrote it down

I remember your aprons
Your doll collection in the cabinet
All with names
Tomasita, Ernestina, Milagro
All mended with spare limbs
All in dresses made of manteles and socks

I remember your hard bed
ten feet from the stove
the bridge to la cocina
rosaries and novenas de santos at your bedside
bottles of Tejuino hidden underneath

I know nothing but warm and sweetness from you
I know your rough hands cupping my face
I know your perfume of smoke, tierra, and pinol
I have questions for you

You know what it's like to be left by a man
High-and-dry, heartbroken, indignant.
How did you deal by yourself?
Did you drink that booze the way I smoke weed?
Did you ever heal by yourself?
My mom has so much fear... so do I
Help me figure out where we got it

Affirmations for Aurelio

When you stayed with us
You always walked me to school
You taught how to jaywalk
Nah! Ese botón es decoración, mija

You made friends with everyone we passed
El paltero always had paleta de sandias for me
Teachers, janitors, and classmate's moms
they always asked about you, Abuelito.
Were you leaving me guardian angels?

I've seen you in my dad's smile
In the way he makes small talk
En como le gusta trabajar
A mi me gusta trabajar too
You taught me not to fear
the smell of my own sweat

Diana Medina

Alchemy

I grew tired of trying to fit into boxes
just so my culture could understand me
just so I could have something in common with my elders
just so they could stay comfortable
just so I could stay "in my place"
just so they could tell me "you are one of us"

That pursuit filled me
with anxiety claiming to be acceptance
That life drowned me
in pressure masquerading as protection
Those expectations overwhelmed me
with toxicity calling itself tradition

Eventually, I broke free
I choose life
I choose healing
I choose cycle breaking
I choose amor propio
I choose to cross a new border

I will transform things
I will turn what needs to be created into purpose
what needs to be said into poetry
what needs to be healed into peace
what needs to be grieved into power

I will shout, "no estoy sola, estoy libre"
From ceilings, roofs, and mountain tops
like an angry rage-filled prayer
A powerful affirmation demanding that
loved ones stop feeling sorry for me
I was blessed with a fresh start,

a clean break, a new chance
to design the life I wanted
in the first place, the life that called to me
when I was too busy being stuck in boxes
to recognize it as my truth.
I will not make that mistake again.

Ode to Mi Diosa

Oh... my... goddess
You're like esas ninas mi Ama told me
not to hang out with in high school because
Dime con quién andas y de dire quién eres
She called them *pobres criaturas perdularias*
If I am with you, entonces quién   soy yo?
Soy todo lo que eres... love and fire

As a little girl, you were the buffet of knowledge
where we refused to eat, elders were too scared
to serve themselves heaping plates of you
Mi cultura me tenia a dieta, I was starving
Now, I fill my plate with your deliciousness
You nourish me with your divinity, your blood
Your ebbs, your flows, your magic...
Your tacos of perspective... I feast on them

Your bathwater smells like roses and
tastes like all the wettest parts of me
I drink it con gusto like Horchata on a hot day
I know what buttons to push on me because
you're on a first name basis with my fingers
You tell me when it's time start typing,
start cooking, start creating, start healing

You are sweetness covered in humor,
surrounded by fire, grounded by earth
Tu no tienes orilla ni fin, You are possibilities
You are bendiciones on a Tuesday afternoon
my sustenance, my fuel, a bold sign that says,
"this woman is a temple so bow motherfuckers"
The Bible never taught me that I am you
You are living, breathing, creating
Thanks to you *soy una criatura divina*

Speak

Belly swollen
Full of words unsaid

Rows full of listening ears
Scary like monsters under the bed

The mic...my lips
A tongue that won't move

I hope my voice will find me
Before El Cucuy does

Work in Progress

I wish I could just let it all go…
Detach: let it all leave me,
make it all feel soothed,
walk away, forget all that heartache.

Each time I think of it I cry less and less.
Maybe that is a start. Maybe it takes practice.
Maybe that is all I can do at this moment
slowly and steadily release that sadness.

I wish I could wake up one day
and proclaim I am healed.
Healed is not a place; it's a journey
I don't think I will ever be done with.

For now, I just let the triggers come
I surrender when they make me ache.
I remember that this peace, these tears,
are healthier than any toxic situation.

Coming Home

change clothes, get comfy
go from covered to naked
let skin finally breathe
enjoy cool breeze kissing skin

hair releases from hair tie
curls cascade on shoulders
hands raise high over head
legs extend in all directions

inhale the sweet silence
dance to solitary symphony
contently utter affirmation:
this space is mine all mine

Diana Medina

Gratitude Revolution

There is fire under my feet
It's hot and making me dance
I jump from side to side
Until I realize the real message:
Stop jumping, start walking
This is not a place for me anymore

Put all fragmented memories
in the old houses I played in
Set fire to those chapters
Watch them all burn down
Watch the smoke fill the sky
with pretty love-shaped clouds
floating off into the ether
cleansing my past, making a way
bestowing me with infinite wisdom
moving me towards the light

The wind whispers in my ear:
Lo que paso, ya paso, Mija
It's over, it's over, it's over…

I am new, I am reborn
I am held, protected,
destined, blessed,
highly favored, loved,
guided by the divine
It will make me stronger,
Make me whole, keep me worthy
It's working… it's working… it's working

No more fronting
No more comparing
No more anger
Just me, my heart, my essence
Saying thank you, thank you, thank you

Healing Out Loud

Diana Medina

About the Author

Diana Medina is a first-generation Mexican-American poet and educator born and raised in Los Angeles, CA. Her mission in life is to use her gift with words to bring more clarity, compassion, and comic relief to the world. She believes that this is how she will leave the world better than she found it. Diana's writing has been featured by Modern Latina Magazine and Story Center. She has also performed at Da Poetry Lounge, The Sacramento Comedy Spot, Borderlands Theater, Sacramento Poetry Center, Capital Storytelling, and Yuba Sutter Art Gallery.

Diana holds a Bachelor's degree in Political Science from California State University, Northridge and a Master's degree in Public Administration from the University of Southern California. She is the Founder and Chief Merriment Officer of Off The Clocker, a company that provides poetic interventions for an ever-changing world in the form of events, micro-coaching, consulting services, inspirational merchandise, publications, and performances. She is also the Program Director at The Practice Space, a Bay Area nonprofit that seeks to build confidence and community through communication skill development programs that advance inclusion, develop empathy, and elevate underrepresented voices for people of all ages. She is trained in storytelling, stand up comedy, and improv, all of which she brings into her poetry and education work.

Diana is the daughter of Mexican immigrant parents, Jose and Natalia Medina. She is the youngest of their 8 children. She is a Tia to 22 nieces and nephews who she loves dearly. Diana enjoys pop culture, poetry, cooking, coffee, puns, thrift stores, knitting, hip hop, home decor, and her huge hilarious family; all of which she has a poem or story about. When she is not writing or working Diana enjoys taking road trips with her furbaby Kika, a chihuahua she named after her Abuelita.

www.ingramcontent.com/pod-product-compliance
Lightning Source LLC
Chambersburg PA
CBHW072150100526
44589CB00015B/2169